"*Lord Acton: Historian and Mora*  important and least rememb
How the thought of Lord A bite about power and corruption should be of great concern to those of us who cherish liberty and human dignity. Why would the West or the church allow such devolution and degradation of Acton's thought? This volume not only puts the brakes on this historical trajectory, but it might also very well begin reversing it."

BRADLEY J. BIRZER
Russell Amos Kirk Chair in American Studies
Professor of History
Hillsdale College

"Gregg's masterful collection gives us Acton in full: liberal, Catholic, historian, moralist, and profound thinker on liberty and its roots. The essays here give us the resources both to consider Acton's work itself, and to inspire us to continue his work in defending liberty into the future."

GERALD RUSSELLO
Editor
The University Bookman

"This far-reaching compendium of essays clearly explains and assesses Lord Acton's productive career and profound contributions as moral historian, philosopher, political theorist, and theologian. This collection is vastly significant in helping modern audiences come to grips with the Christian foundations undergirding the concept of liberty, and it is necessary reading for all citizens living in a free society."

JOHN D. WILSEY
Assistant Professor of History and Christian Apologetics
Southwestern Baptist Theological Seminary

"Lord Acton is not well-known today. His emphasis on the uniqueness of Western civilization and on the great role of Christianity in the history of liberty do not suit the dominant mood of today's academia and the prevailing narrative served to the public. He is thus often casually dismissed or doomed to oblivion. Yet Acton, an avid student of Burke and Tocqueville, had a no less penetrating mind than these great thinkers. This collection of articles on Acton helps to uncover the many treasures in Acton's writings and therefore renders a great service to students of politics and to all who search for wisdom."

CHRISTOPHER LAZARSKI
Author of *Power Tends to Corrupt: Lord Acton's Study of Liberty*

HISTORIAN AND MORALIST

HISTORIAN AND MORALIST

EDITED BY SAMUEL GREGG

ACTON INSTITUTE

ACTONINSTITUTE

98 E. Fulton
Grand Rapids, Michigan 49503
Phone: 616.454.3080
Fax: 616.454.9454
www.acton.org

Interior composition: Judy Schafer
Cover: Scaturro Design

Printed in the United States of America

CONTENTS

ABBREVIATIONS

Add. Mss.
Additional Manuscripts. Acton Papers. Cambridge University Library.

CLARS
The Correspondence of Lord Acton and Richard Simpson. 3 vols. Edited by Josef L. Altholz, Damian McElrath, and James C. Holland. Cambridge: Cambridge University Press, 1971–75.

Correspondence
Selections from the Correspondence of the First Lord Acton. Edited by John Neville Figgis and Reginald Vere Laurence. London: Longmans, Green, and Co., 1917.

LFR
Lectures on the French Revolution. Edited by John Neville Figgis and Reginald Vere Laurence. London: Macmillan, 1920.

LMH
Lectures on Modern History. Edited by John Neville Figgis and Reginald Vere Laurence. London: Macmillan, 1907.

SW
Selected Writings of Lord Acton. 3 vols. Edited by J. Rufus Fears. Indianapolis: Liberty Fund, 1985–88.

INTRODUCTION

Samuel Gregg

John Emerich Edward Dalberg Acton, First Baron Acton (1834–1902), was perhaps one of the most enigmatic figures of Victorian England. Politically speaking, he was a strong Liberal, or, perhaps more precisely, a Whig for all his adult life. Yet he was also one of Europe's most well-known Roman Catholics. In many ways a quintessential English eccentric, Acton was equally comfortable with high German intellectual culture. Widely regarded as one of the most learned men of his time, Acton penned very little by way of academic articles, let alone books. For much of his life, Acton's closest friend was his intellectual mentor, Father Ignaz von Döllinger (1799–1890). Acton declined, however, to follow Döllinger's path after the First Vatican Council and, unlike his friend, went to great lengths in order to successfully avoid excommunication over the dogma of papal infallibility. A man always willing to speak his mind on other occasions, much of Acton's life is accurately described as marked by drift—as if he never quite found his niche, whether as a historian, a politician, or layman active in Catholic affairs.

For all this ambiguity, however, a constant was Acton's commitment to the cause of liberty. Much of his life's work was devoted to exploring how it was the case that societies characterized by freedom emerged in Europe and the West more generally rather than elsewhere. In many books that trace the development of Western civilization, "the birth of freedom" is often identified with the various Enlightenments. Certainly, the Enlightenment made contributions to human liberty that Christians would not wish to do without. Nonetheless, Acton did not believe that serious appreciation and promotion of freedom and its moral and institutional supports were somehow dormant until the late seventeenth century.

Any discussion of freedom and Christianity quickly surfaces the numerous instances in which Christians have undermined human liberty. Reference is invariably made to the various Inquisitions, the witch trials conducted by Puritans, forced conversions, and other instances of intolerance. Acton never denied that Christians and Christian institutions have on many occasions violated the rightful freedoms of others. Indeed, if anything, he belabored the point. This, however, did not prevent Acton from maintaining that it was, for the most part, Christianity that provided the moral, theological, and cultural principles upon which Christians and others have drawn to condemn unjust coercion. It may well be that Acton did not believe that liberalism could have arrived at such conclusions without these deeper background influences.

For Acton, this was more than an attempt to make an empirical case that linked particular cultures and religions with the rise of liberty. Acton believed in liberty and its growth as something good in itself—so much so that he was willing to commit his life to its protection and furtherance from any quarter from which he believed it was threatened. That included any challenge that, in his view, emerged from among his coreligionists. For most of Acton's life, it is worth remembering, liberty and religion, but especially the Catholic religion, were seen in continental Europe as being at odds: something that, as Acton's contemporary Alexis de Tocqueville famously stated, was not replicated in the America visited by Acton in 1853, twenty-two years after Tocqueville's more famous voyage to the New World.

It would be a grave mistake, however, to conceive Acton's thinking about this matter as being driven by an instinct to place religion and freedom at odds. On the contrary, Acton wanted to reestablish and build what he saw as a natural alliance between Christianity and the forces of freedom. Liberty, he believed, could not be properly understood without grasping its fundamental roots in, first, Judaism and then Christianity. The pre-Christian Greco-Roman world could never, Acton believed, have birthed the idea of freedom. There was something distinct about Christianity that, as Acton saw it, made liberty what it was. Ongoing conflict between the world of liberty and Christianity, especially the Catholic Church, was good for neither. This is quite removed from the notion that liberalism is the answer to which Christianity was the problem.

All the papers contained in this collected volume seek to address the many contradictions in Acton's life but also discuss at some length Acton's ongoing personal and intellectual wrestling with the theme of religion and freedom. Some of the most interesting of Acton's reflections on these matters occurred toward the end of his life, most notably during his time as the chair of modern history at the University of Cambridge—an institution that was closed to him in the earlier part of his life on account of Acton's Catholicism. This period in Acton's life is covered in detail by Owen Chadwick in the first paper contained in this collection. Much of Chadwick's analysis focuses on revealing the man behind the very formal exterior: the lecturer who could be very tough on his students but who also urged them not to be intimidated by his manner and demanding standards.

Chadwick also explores Acton's distinctly "moralistic" approach to the study of history. By "moralistic" is meant the habit of making moral judgments about historical figures and institutions. To that end, Chadwick outlines what he regards as the principles that Acton brought to the process of making such judgments, some of which may surprise readers or which have received less attention than others.

Acton himself has not been exempt from judgment. His idea of liberalism is explored and critiqued in depth by Johann Christian Koecke. Having highlighted the many incongruities in Acton's life, Koecke asks searching questions such as whether anyone can be a liberal (depending on what is meant by this term) and a Catholic at the same time. He also notes that Acton was enthralled by "the big picture" and grand historical themes, at the very time when much of the historical profession (especially in the German-speaking world) was becoming increasingly focused on the miniscule and suspicious of all-encompassing narratives. The larger question examined by Koecke is whether Acton produced a theory of liberalism and, if so, if it constitutes a coherent set of principles. He proceeds to consider Acton's treatment of a number of principles—such as freedom of thought,

freedom of conscience, and the need to limit power—typically identified as "liberal." Koecke's somewhat depressing conclusion is that
democracy, especially the social democracy that is so widespread in
Europe, has increasingly resulted in a squeezing-out and marginaliza-
tion of these principles identified by Acton.

Christoph Böhr brings us closer to Acton's philosophical convictions about the nature of freedom. Even though, Böhr stresses, Acton
was not a philosopher, the very process of exploring the history of
liberty forced Acton to wrestle with the meaning of the word *liberty*
and its implications for social and political order. For Acton, Böhr
argues, "freedom is the assurance that everyone is protected to do
what they believe they ought to do." He further maintains that this
conviction led Acton to adopt a quite skeptical view of the state and
state power. This is especially true when it comes to Acton's view of
the state's role vis-à-vis religion, which is to foster the independence
of religion. It follows that religion in turn becomes the guarantee of
liberty from arbitrary state power. It was especially important for
Acton, Böhr maintains, that people's ability to freely choose to obey
God is preserved from arbitrary actions on the part of the government.

Throughout his essay, Böhr teases out the ways in which Acton
sought to illustrate how religion, the state, and liberty are linked to
and, given the right conditions, can support one another. Certainly,
the balance is delicate and never quite right. Böhr states, however, that
it is through these tensions that many limits to the power of religion
and the state are established. He also illustrates that Acton's account
of this process has been affirmed by prominent contemporary historians of religious and philosophical ideas, such as the French Catholic
thinker Rémi Brague. Like Koecke, Böhr believes that Acton's attention to the potential for the tyranny of the majority is something worth
heeding today, both in terms of preserving religious liberty and for
maintaining firm limits on state power.

Josef L. Altholz returns the reader to exploration of the theme of
Acton as a historian. Affirming the insight that Acton's approach is
essentially one of a moralist, Altholz emphasizes just how connected
this concern is to Acton's conviction that "liberty of historical thought
and writing was founded on religious principles, the moral obligation of truthfulness, and the sanctity of truth." Aware of how foreign
this surely sounds to the ears of a good number of historians today,

Altholz argues that Acton's reputation as a "historian and moralist" owes much to the influences of the Victorian period in which the word "Truth" was invariably (and refreshingly) capitalized. Such truth demands, by definition, freedom of inquiry. But Acton's emphasis on these matters, Altholz holds, reflects also the influence of Döllinger, and the latter's steady move away from historical apologetics toward an emphasis on intellectual freedom, especially from ecclesiastical authority.

This is not to portray Acton and Döllinger as foreshadowing twentieth-century theologians such as Hans Küng, whom, it might be argued, moved from defending intellectual liberty toward rebellion for the sake, it seems, of disruption. Rather, Altholz believes that they were concerned with ensuring that imprudent and even evil choices by church authorities were not hidden by historians whose loyalty was to institutions rather than the Truth. Ultimately, Acton's positions on these matters, Altholz comments, were so strong that they contributed to a breakdown in his relationship with Döllinger when the latter was more willing to defend Bishop Félix Dupanloup, a "liberal" who, after opposing the definition of papal infallibility at Vatican I, supported the council's quite qualified, even restrictive definition of the controversial dogma. To this, Altholz adds that Acton never seemed to realize that the study of history is as much (if not more) about context as it is about texts. But Altholz also maintains that Acton's effort to establish "the historian as judge" was bound to fail. Toward the end of his life, Acton seems to have accepted that his colleagues, being human, could aim, at best, for objectivity or, to use Acton's preferred word, "impartiality."

The paper penned by Rudolf Uertz moves us from Acton's ideas about liberty and history toward Acton as a theoretician of politics. Noting the common and, to an extent, verifiable link between Christianity and conservative politics, Uertz underscores that Acton was somewhat of an anomaly in asserting a strong link, and even the possibility of an alliance between Christianity and liberalism. According to Uertz, the way to understand Acton's ideas about politics is through careful attention to his ideas about the relationship between church and state (especially in light of his activities during the First Vatican Council), and his view of democracy and constitutional order.

Acton, Uertz maintains, drew upon Greek thought and Christianity when developing his view of ethics: the inadequacies of antiquity being corrected, in Acton's view, by the Christian religion, especially with regard to the crucial topic of liberty, of which freedom of conscience is seen as a central part. Christianity's vital distinction between the temporal and spiritual realms provided the vital ingredient that Stoicism could not furnish. In this regard, Uertz suggests that Acton's view of the state was shaped by an outlook and focus quite different from the way that the Catholic Church, under the impetus of the revival of natural-law theory in the nineteenth century, developed its thinking on the nature of the state, church-state relations, and the social question: all of which were to strongly influence Catholic political movements in continental Europe. Uertz illustrates that Acton's emphasis on the ways in which legal and political systems develop to limit and eventually undo state absolutism reflect a historian's attention to the unfolding of events and ideas over time. This is one of the reasons why, Uertz states, Acton had a rather positive view of the American Revolution.

Stephen Tonsor points out that there is something highly intriguing about someone from as high a continental European aristocratic background as Acton being such an admirer of America and devotee of liberty. Liberty was, for many Catholic aristocrats, associated strongly with the violence and disorder of the French Revolution. Part of the puzzle, Tonsor maintains, is explained by the fact that Acton was exposed to English Whigs, such as his stepfather the Second Earl Granville, and Whig ideas from an early age. More generally, however, it was Acton's commitment to liberty and his understanding of how free societies had emerged over time that, according to Tonsor, disposed him to think well of the United States. Religion and the rights of conscience play a major role in Tonsor's account. Part of this has to do with Acton's association of particular expressions of Protestantism with absolutism, and his attention to the fact that English Catholics were among the first to insist upon, and establish, a relatively expansive understanding of religious liberty in the Maryland colony. Another is Acton's conviction that the American Revolution reflected a shift away from arguments about the rights of Englishmen to the rights found in a higher law that transcended nationality.

Tonsor argues that Acton was perhaps the most perceptive observer of America among nineteenth century historians. So why have his insights into America been neglected by historians? Tonsor's answer is that Acton supported the Confederate cause in the Civil War, or what Acton called the "second American Revolution." This advocacy, Tonsor argues, needs to be understood against a background of the rise of nationalism and centralization and the growth of bureaucracy that, in Acton's view, were undermining the cause of liberty and liberalism in continental Europe, especially in what would become Imperial Germany. To the extent that America was drifting away from states' rights and federalism, it was following the same trend. Acton's support for the South thus had nothing to do with slavery, which he abhorred. Still, Tonsor notes, it is striking that Acton, as an outspoken advocate of moral absolutes, tended to portray slavery as something that needed to be viewed as part of particular historical circumstances—a position he did not adopt toward other subjects.

Other apparent contradictions in Acton's thought are explored by Russell Kirk in his paper on Acton's view of revolutions. This lecture was one of the very last (if not the last) public lectures given by Kirk before his death in 1994. Though Acton lived in a world untouched by the disorder and violence of revolution, Kirk argues that Acton's writings repeatedly commend revolutionary upheaval. Sometimes this is revolution in the realm of ideas, but it also extends, Kirk maintains, to often quite violent political revolutions.

Kirk stresses that Acton spoke highly of Edmund Burke on many occasions and underscores Acton's shock at the violent anticlericalism of the Paris Commune of 1870. The key to understanding how Acton combined these ideas and sentiments with a general approval of revolutionary change was Acton's belief that such upheavals tended to promote greater liberty, understood as freedom from arbitrary power as well as the capacity to fulfill freely one's moral duties. In retrospect, Kirk suggests, this seems a little naïve, especially in light of the Bolshevik Revolution in Russia and the misery and destruction brought in the wake of revolutionary movements in Europe, Asia, and Latin America throughout the twentieth century. Kirk also maintains that, on the subject of revolution, Acton's thought became more radical and less prudent as time passed and less Burkean in its understanding of revolution. This seems, according to Kirk, to contradict Acton's animus against the notion that the end justifies the means.

James Holland takes us away from some of these more specific controversies surrounding Acton and immerses us in the full canopy of influences that shaped Acton's outlook as a Catholic, a liberal, and a historian. It was, Holland suggests, a blessing in disguise that Acton was rejected by three Cambridge colleges on account of his Catholicism and forced, instead, to seek learning in continental Europe.

As a result of this development, Acton came into contact with not only Döllinger but also the lesser-known philologist and politician Peter Ernst von Lasaulx (1805–1861). It was the latter who introduced Acton to the notion of ideas having a history and the possibility of studying the development of ideas through time as a historian. Holland also focuses on the influence of the historian Leopold von Ranke (1795–1886) on Acton, especially with regard to Acton's interest in history as a *science*—something about which Döllinger had significant reservations on account of the secularist presuppositions built into particular conceptions of the nature of science. Without this "Germanic" learning and influences, Holland holds, Acton would not have been able to play the role that he did at the First Vatican Council.

Even more significant, Holland maintains, is that Acton found himself immersed in the rising historical theology that characterized German Catholic intellectual life during this period. Originally conceived as an exercise in apologetics, the historical theology developed by Döllinger and others led to an insistence on the need for free intellectual inquiry, one that could not be bound by the claims of ecclesiastical authority. Concerning the latter, Holland points out that the sensitivity of ecclesiastical reactions to claims for intellectual autonomy reflected, in part, the growing antireligious sentiments often associated with such movements in nineteenth century Europe.

The last paper in this collection takes the reader back to the central passion of Acton's intellectual life—the concern for liberty—and the way it relates to Acton's view of the nature of social and political order. My focus is on Acton's understanding of, first, the relationship between political liberty and democracy, and, second, the relationship between political liberty and Christianity. Acton, I suggest, was not against democracy *per se* and argued that the spread of democracy in the ancient world generally (though not always) helped the cause of liberty. Nevertheless Acton was deeply worried about the potential for tyrannies of the majority: something that has always concerned liberals of an Actonian stripe.

The difficulty facing the ancient world vis-à-vis liberty, Acton maintained, concerned its inability to recognize any authority higher than the state. Herein, I claim, is the most lasting significance of Christianity for liberty, at least when it comes to protecting freedom from over-mighty governments. It is also the way, I maintain, to understand the interplay between two of Acton's most famous papers, "The History of Freedom in Antiquity" (February 1877) and "The History of Freedom in Christianity" (May 1877). The growth of liberty becomes understood, from Acton's standpoint, as providential insofar as the ancient world could never have managed to arrive at a mature idea of liberty under its own volition. It took God's entry as a person into the course of human history for the desacralization of the state, always implicit in the Hebrew Scriptures, to begin in earnest. Unlike a good number of Acton's contributions to historical reflection, there is no ambiguity about this point in Acton's thought.

Taken together, this collection of papers illustrates that, for all the absence of a great work penned by Acton, his scattered writings, correspondence, and notes provide readers with much to ponder. Linking all these contributions is the conviction that Acton was painfully aware of the delicacy and rareness of liberty, and how easily it could be pulverized by arbitrary power from without, or hollowed out from within by an abandonment of moral absolutes. This was not especially well understood by a good number of his contemporaries, whether they were his fellow liberals or his fellow Catholics. Such insights, however, remain pertinent today, more than a century after Acton's death in 1902. For all the debates about the changes and ambiguities in Acton's thought, Acton's willingness to defend freedom remains the great constant that we can continue to admire and remember today.

1

PROFESSOR LORD ACTON*

Owen Chadwick

On 13 January 1895 the regius professor of history at Cambridge, Sir John Seeley, died. Acton, though he had no book to his name, was one of the famous historians in England, by reason of the articles which he had written and his help in founding the *English Historical Review*. He had no experience of teaching, young or old. But his learning was rare and respected in what was then coming to be, for the first time, the profession of historians. So in himself he was considerable. He worked exceptionally hard at books. For example in 1893: when he was in Oxford he spent nine hours a day at the Bodleian Library. In London he worked hours at the British Museum where they kept looking for the books he wanted from Paris or Leipzig and gave him "a table in a snug corner with about 100 volumes on it, mostly uncut" where he worked daily until darkness fell, and then he moved to the Athenaeum and continued with another pile of books waiting there.[1]

---

*Originally given as a lecture at Cambridge University in March 1995 celebrating the centennial of Lord Acton's appointment to the Regius Chair of Modern History. Reprinted from Owen Chadwick, *Acton and History* (Cambridge: Cambridge University Press, 1998), 204–45, with permission from Cambridge University Press.

[1] Acton to Annie, 15 December 1893, no. 72.

He had thought himself possible as an Oxford professor of history when the chair there was vacant in 1894; and he would not have imagined things for himself which were out of the realm of the practical.

THE APPOINTMENT OF ACTON

The Cambridge University Calendar for 1894–5 said that the regius professor of history must be a Master of Arts, or of Law, or of a superior degree. This was understood at the time to mean that he must hold a degree from the university of Cambridge. If that was right, it ruled out Acton; he had applied to be an undergraduate at Cambridge, to three different colleges (Magdalene was one, his uncle was there) and was not admitted. From the University of Cambridge he received an honorary doctorate in 1888 and the question was raised whether an honorary doctorate counted for this purpose. So now the statute appeared to exclude him as a possible professor. The same statute appeared to exclude other great names whom Cambridge might want—the name of S. R. Gardiner of *England under the Earlier Stuarts* was mentioned at Cambridge, but apart from the blot of his Oxford origin he had refused the Oxford regius chair the previous year. The name of Thomas Hodgkin, of *Italy and her Invaders*, was talked about in Cambridge but he bore the still worse blot of being a graduate of London. The principal of Newnham, who was Gladstone's youngest daughter Helen, proposed both these eminent names.

None other than Vinogradoff was suggested by Pollock on the ground that he was unhappy in Tsarist Russia but he had the blot that he was a graduate of Moscow. Vinogradoff did not finally settle in England, because his liberal opinions were not acceptable in St Petersburg, until the year before Acton died, and he became a professor at Oxford the year after Acton died.

There were some bad ideas. Two obscure persons without any history in them wanted the job because of their political services to the Liberal Party, and were not ashamed to plead that case.

There was an excellent Cambridge teacher of history George Prothero; but he had only lately accepted the chair at Edinburgh and it was thought impossible for the Crown to try to shift him back so quickly; especially when the principal adviser to the Queen was so eminent a Scot.

So must it be someone now teaching in Cambridge? Mandell Creighton, who surprised everyone when he left his chair at Cambridge for the see of Peterborough, said, "Really there is no one now at Cambridge except Gwatkin [Creighton's successor as the professor of ecclesiastical history] who can be said to know any history."

But there was one person in Cambridge who thought he was learned in history and wanted the chair, even thought it justice that he should have it: Oscar Browning, Fellow of King's, famous in the world as a character. This was the cause of panic. All the local people were determined to do their utmost to avert the fate of having Browning as their professor.

Before Seeley died Browning was already planning to succeed him. As soon as Seeley died Browning wrote to the Prime Minister asking to be appointed; and the Royal Archives at Windsor show that his application went higher than the Prime Minister. Browning had a claim and a disadvantage. He was a good teacher of history to undergraduates; and had done something to help found the History Tripos. His disadvantage was that he was the most inaccurate man ever to hold a Cambridge lectureship in history. The apocryphal story about him was that he wrote a book on Frederick the Great of Prussia and everyone was surprised to find him devoting so much military history to the conquest of Siberia; and that afterwards the book had an erratum slip, *wherever Siberia occurs please read Silesia.* He was also an eccentric. He had a huge stomach on very small legs, and the only hairs he had were wavy curls round the collar. But professors may look how they like, and eccentricity is not a quality which is a disadvantage to Cambridge historians who had the poet Gray as their professor. Not so long before, they had Professor Smyth. He was said to give the same course of lectures every year, which was possible because no one came; except when he came to the lecture on Marie Antoinette, to which many people came, to see the professor weep, which he did every year.[2]

Browning admired Acton. He was a member of the Liberal Party and Acton was one of the handful of Liberal peers in the House of Lords. He revered persons with titles and Acton satisfied that affecta-

---

[2] Leslie Stephen's reminiscence, given to Prothero, Prothero's Diary, 5 October 1902, King's College.

3

tion. He used to send Acton his articles and Acton kindly corrected the elementary mistakes in them. Four years earlier Browning had tried to get King's College to elect Acton as a fellow. When Mandell Creighton left Cambridge to be Bishop of Peterborough, Browning tried to persuade Acton to stand as a possible professor of church history; and Acton the Roman Catholic replied, "I should not satisfy the requirements as a teacher of Protestant doctrine."[3] So when Seeley died, Browning and Acton were close, well known to each other. Acton, who knew a historian when he saw one, did not value Browning as a historian but as his link with Cambridge; Browning valued Acton as a historian and a peer and a Liberal.

The best and the worst that can be said for Oscar Browning came in letters that month to the Prime Minister. The best was from a Kingsman:

> The work he has done amongst the younger men is remarkable. He has devoted his time and thrown open his rooms to them from all colleges, and has given conversational lectures to them round his fireside on periods of history, leading them to take an interest in history as throwing light on present day questions, in a way that no one else I have known at Cambridge has done.

And the worst: Henry Jackson the great Greek scholar reported to Harcourt of the panic lest Browning might get it. The words were the stronger because Jackson was a man of such sympathy. "It is suggested that if he should be appointed there would be two consequences, (1) disaster to the history school (2) disaster to liberalism."[4]

On 11 February 1895 the Vice-Chancellor, Austen-Leigh, pointed out to the Prime Minister that the axiom was false. The professor had not the least need to be a Cambridge graduate. It used to be so. But in 1861 this statute was repealed. They took a couple of legal opinions to make sure. But before the judge replied, the Prime Minister acted.

---

[3] Acton to Browning, 6 March 1891; cf. *Correspondence*, 70.

[4] Pro, R. P. Edgcumbe to Rosebery, 2 February 1895; against, Henry Jackson to Harcourt, 24 January 1895; in Rosebery Papers, National Library of Scotland, 1051/138 and 185.

Acton was large in Rosebery's mind. They were colleagues in the Liberal party. Acton had tried to persuade Rosebery to send him as ambassador to Bavaria, where was his family's home; without success. Rosebery knew that Acton's financial affairs had been going awry and that he needed a stipend. And he found that some in Cambridge, Henry Sidgwick for example, wanted Acton as professor.

On 15 February 1895 Acton wrote to Rosebery accepting the offer of the chair.

Acton to Oscar Browning 18 February 1895:

> I am sorry to be the bearer of strange and unexpected news. It has occurred to Lord Rosebery to offer the professorship to me. Of course I at once told him that I could not entertain or consider a proposal if I was to stand in your way; but I learned that he had been advised to prefer several other candidates in case of a refusal, and that there would be no chance the offer would be made to you. I know not whom he has consulted. The only friend of mine whom he has taken into counsel advised that I should not be appointed—I presume on religious grounds. I mention this that you may be assured I have not put myself forward, but that no friends of mine have employed their influence in my favour to the detriment of your obvious claims ...

After Acton was appointed Browning welcomed him most kindly and they remained friends of a curious sort. He even wrote to the Prime Minister saying how much he welcomed Acton. But inside Browning remained bitter that no one made him the professor, and he imagined mysterious unknown foes writing false information to the Prime Minister to do him down. Foes did write about him but the information was not all false.

Gladstone was the person not pleased at the appointment. Gladstone wanted Acton's mind on wider fields and thought that to go to a chair at Cambridge would be a narrowing of what he could contribute.[5] Gladstone sounded slightly surprised that otherwise the approval seemed to have been unanimous, for he would have expected bigotry to object to a Roman Catholic being put into such a post. His

---

[5] Gladstone to Acton, 27 February 1895, mutilated letter.

daughter Mary gave three cheers for the appointment.[6] Gladstone warned him that not all would be well in Cambridge because there is an "organized group or section of Low Churchmen under a Mr Moule."[7]

Why was Acton appointed? (1) S. R. Gardiner wanted to write his book. (2) Mandell Creighton had gone away to be a bishop. (3) Thomas Hodgkin had no desire to work in a university and wanted to finish his book. (4) The Prime Minister was liberal and so was Acton. (5) Acton needed paid work, not so easy for a peer in those days. (6) Since an unlearned person inside the university had certain claims even though he had earned some contempt, it was absolutely necessary to bring in a very learned person from outside the university. And (7), it was possible to appoint a Roman Catholic for the first time because the liberal governments had slowly opened public offices to members of every denomination; and this particular Roman Catholic was acceptable to Protestants because on his record he was thought to be not in favour of Popes. The Queen commented on the friendly way he was received at Cambridge—"what a happy change there has been"; and Acton the courtier replied to her, "All due, Ma'am, to your Majesty's reign."[8]

Not all the London intelligentsia were pleased and had an excuse to say what they thought when he started to lecture. They used strong language: "an overpowering deluge of verbiage." "One catches here and there sentences with gleams of light in them" "hope he will resign the chair for which he is in no way qualified." "Surely one of the indispensable qualifications for the chair of Modern History at Cambridge is that its occupant should be intelligible."[9]

Acton's first official act was to read a dissertation and advise Cambridge not to print it. He looked for lodgings and found a place like a warren full of students in straw hats and rejected it. He found the Master of Trinity College almost too gushing and his able much younger wife very pleasant indeed. Trinity Hall offered him

---

[6] Mary Drew to Acton, 19 February 1895.

[7] This is Handley Moule, a sweet-natured, non-obstreperous person, afterwards a vague but beloved Bishop of Durham.

[8] Acton to Annie, no. 105.

[9] *Spectator*, 15 June 1895, p. 814; *Saturday Review*, 89 (1895), 822.

a Fellowship but he refused it and preferred to be given rooms at Trinity. He described how "a funny old woman" took care of him and that he had a manservant, an ex-soldier, and he thought it worthy of note that he bore a moustache.

He loved being at Cambridge. He loved being a Cambridge man "at last." Some thought these years the happiest of his life. He had been an academic *manqué* and now was no longer *manqué*. Trinity elected him to an honorary Fellowship and he moved into rooms in Nevile's court. Later, as the number of books grew and grew, Trinity added the next door room to his.

THE INAUGURAL LECTURE

He realised that his conception of history was different from Seeley's. Seeley thought that history is politics. Acton said very early that history is not the history of politics—why not? politics pass. "History compels us to fasten on abiding issues, and rescues us from the temporary and transient." We need to share the existence of societies not our own.

He gave his Inaugural Lecture on 11 June 1895. It was the most famous Inaugural Lecture ever given. It was a calamity for professors because it meant afterwards that they all had to think of giving inaugural lectures. It was an utterance so rare, in places so profound, and in other places so personal, that it can be read again and again without boring the reader. He took the chance to state not only his attitude to history and the past but his philosophy of life and moral being. For unlike most historians he thought that a person's attitude to history and his philosophy of life and morality are not two different attitudes but are the same.

Afterwards he showed his weaker side by adding to the published version too many pages of footnotes. The lecture was printed in seventy-four pages, the notes in fifty-seven; but the smaller print of the notes meant that there were many words more than in the lecture.

The love of unnecessary footnotes is a notorious sin of professors because they are suspected, not of ensuring that the reader can see the sources which justify what they said, but of wishing the world to think that they are encyclopaedias on two feet. But these footnotes were different. During the lecture he stated various historical facts, though not a heap of them; a few of which might be argued about.

The notes made no attempt to justify this information from their sources. The notes are extracts from writers whose opinions were like or nearly like Acton's. He had spent years compiling an index of remarkable quotations and the temptation to empty the card index into the back pages of his printed lecture was too pressing to resist. The notes to the Inaugural Lecture are the chief pointer, besides his failure to publish, in support of the critics who think he would have done well to throw some of his card index into the dustbin. It is just possible also, that a new professor of history who had not proved to anyone (but experts) that he knew much history, succumbed to the desire to show his new university that at least this incoming incumbent had read shelves and shelves of books.

But the Inaugural was of a far bigger stature than its notes. It had theory and practice. The theory was a coherent summary of Acton's historical ideal. The practice was good advice to students on how to learn history.

But he had other aims in his mind. He needed to show this Protestant audience that a Roman Catholic historian is neither of necessity illiberal nor of necessity bigoted against Protestant sects. He went out of his way to stress these two parts of his personal liberalism. All that century Popes had been condemning liberalism and revolution. Acton sang the praises of the extreme dissenters of the seventeenth century because the religious conscience was the foundation of English democracy. He did not quite sing the praise of revolution but he did say that revolutions had done much good for the human race; we have to face it that we owe good results to violence; we owe religious liberty to the Dutch revolution (he does not say more, but notice the implication against Spanish repression), constitutional government to the English revolution, federal republicanism to the American, political equality to the French "and its successors" (which did he mean?). There was here a contradiction because by its nature revolution breaks with the past and "abolishes history," as some of the French revolutionaries wanted to do. But Acton, observing the contradiction, tried to show that by freeing society from the tighter hold by the past on the present, the revolution made the conditions for a renewal and flowering of historical study.

Then he needed to prove to the university that history is tough, a worthy training of the mind. He found so many of the traditional professors who regarded it as an easy option for young people not good at Latin and Greek and not able to cope with pure mathematics. This severity of history was easy to show but not easy within parts of an hour. He achieved it in two words—*trust nobody*.

The witnesses lie. Or twist the evidence of what happened to suit their cause or their politics or their Church. Or imagine they say what they did not see. Or did not see aright what they saw. Or were so filled with prejudice that they misinterpreted what happened. Or were so ignorant that they misunderstood what they heard. We only have human witnesses and all without exception are wicked or biased. Such is the human condition and such the first vast problem of the historian. *Trust nobody*. Ask their motives. Try to test their sources of information. Examine their background. See what prejudice they might have.

He added to this a doctrine, which his successor and admirer and critic Sir Herbert Butterfield carried to its limit—a Christian is bound to this distrust of the witnesses by his awareness of original sin.

This distrust applies to more than individuals. Governments are worst of all for hiding, manufacturing, altering evidence. Power needs not to tell the truth or only to tell part of it; and to make propaganda; and propaganda is often a lie or an intention to mislead ... in this distrust of the powerful we have a vast advantage over all our predecessors. Modern representative governments have opened their archives and their example has persuaded other States to open their archives. This therefore (he told his audience—and he was right) is a marvellous new age for historical study. For the first time in history we can check from the sources what governments used to say.

Therefore history is not prejudice but the cure of prejudice; not compilation but critical training. The past has no edges and so opens a limitless field of research, in which the method of criticism is scientific and learns from contemporary natural scientists in the use of analysis.

Then this historian who never taught anyone before gave them hints on how to train themselves as historians. Some of these hints became so famous that they are still quoted:

Ideas are more influential than individual people. Study ideas in preference to men and women though the ideas are put forward by men and women. This means that history cannot be "national." No frontier can keep out ideas. By their nature ideas are international. Then history by its nature is international.

Ideas are the cause of what happens, not the effect of what happens. Therefore, in judging the past, we must condemn the theory more harshly than its results.

(Is it right, so invariably? Is it right, the doctrine, we must condemn the theory more than the results? The chief theorist of Nazi racialism was Rosenberg. He was a contemptible whose work made no difference to what happened. Men sublimated their frustrations about society into a hatred of aliens who were alien because they looked different or had different customs; and then the gut-feeling of hatred took hold of the half-literate and they used Rosenberg's *Myth of the Twentieth Century*, and the theory was an accessory to what was hateful, not the cause of the hatred.)

Because ideas are so powerful, there is, he taught, a certain priority in the study of history to ecclesiastical history, the study of religion; for religious ideas have been the most powerful of ideas in social development.

Further advice to young historians included:

we easily fail to see what is already printed somewhere
    but has been forgotten

learn as much by writing as by reading

be not content with the best book—seek sidelights from
    others

have no favourites

see that your judgements are your own

suspect power more than vice

study problems in preference to periods

For this last he gave instances and they were all problems of intellectual history—the origins of the ideas of Luther and Adam Smith and Rousseau, the influence of the scientific ideas of Bacon, the consistency of Burke, the identity of the first Whig.

He said that he understood modern history, the area which he would take as his own, to begin with Christopher Columbus and the Renaissance when scholars first learned how to distinguish genuine documents among the forged so plentiful in the Middle Ages; when history was "full-grown." In the earlier part of the lecture he almost seemed to imply that ancient and medieval history were not worth studying in comparison. He did not wish to include contemporary history because the archives were not yet open and we had less perspective and therefore the result of inquiry must be further from any certainty. But when he came to the practical training of a young historian he took the opposite view about premodern history. The materials for modern history are too vast. We need to start with areas where the sources are limited. Therefore the best training in historical method comes from studying themes or moments in ancient or medieval history. He gave instances—the sources of Plutarch's *Pericles*, the two tracts on Athenian government, the origin of the epistle to Diognetus, the date of the life of St Antony; areas very limited in scope but they all happen to be of rare difficulty for historians whether young or not; and come from the ancient world. And this led him to a general law—gain mastery by taking a small area of study, do not risk superficiality.

The historian cannot be engaged as a politician. The one indispensable quality is detachment. He never mentioned Döllinger as his master though Döllinger had taught him how to be a historian. Twice during the inaugural he talked in praise of Ranke, once he defined him as "my master," once he described his last private visit to the old man; Ranke the practitioner of the ideal of absolute detachment, Ranke who taught historians that it was indispensable to get behind the books to the unpublished records. There is an enchanting Actonian phrase: Ranke taught the modern study of history "to be critical, to be colourless, and new. We meet him at every step and he has done more for us than any other man."

That word *colourless* history was important. The best history was when the historian did not appear in the pages. Not like Macaulay. Not like Thiers. Not like Treitschke. But like Stubbs. Like Fustel de Coulanges. Acton did not practise what he preached. He loved colour. He enjoyed it when he could illustrate the past by personal reminiscence. But in the inaugural he stated the ideal of detachment

11

very persuasively. By the nature of the work the historian ought to be Olympian. It is duty to put at its best the side which the writer personally thinks the wrong cause; and to avoid pertinacity in defending the cause which the writer personally believes to be right. If a Catholic writes a life of Calvin it ought to be impossible for the reader to know from the text that the author is a Catholic. If a patriotic German wrote a Life of Napoleon no one should be able to infer the patriotism from the book.

He seemed to have no use for philosophies of history. He warned his new university against them. But whether or not he had what may be called a philosophy, he worked with two principles which he thought essential and which could hardly be extracted from a study of the past.

The first was that human society is in progress. This progress is observable. Absolutism is finished. He had no idea that forty years after his death all Europe but Britain and Ireland and Switzerland and Sweden and Finland would have absolute governments. If someone had prophesied it he would have found it incredible. Not all is yet done but he was sure that we are moving to civilized societies. What is a civilized society? He defined it:

> representative government
>
> the end of slavery
>
> the security in society of the weaker groups and the minorities
>
> liberty of conscience.

The second general principle was moral, his fight with the unmentioned Döllinger. History is moral judge. We cannot be so detached that we refuse to judge. And when we judge we must not succumb to the temptation of so many past historians of excusing by saying that in those days moral axioms were different. He gave instances—his hero Ranke related how King William III "ordered" the massacre of Glencoe (is it true?)—yet when he sums up the King's character in admiration, murder is not mentioned. Halifax did not believe in the Popish plot but insisted that innocent people should be executed to satisfy the multitude; and then Macaulay wrote of Halifax as of a forgiving and compassionate temper. Beware of the historian's whitewash. We must have the ideal of detachment, but not absolutely, because we are the conscience of the human race about its past. That is why history is a moral education as well as intellectual training. So he came to his famous end—"if we lower our standard in history, we cannot uphold it in Church or State."

THE LECTURES IN THE FACULTY

Professors needed to lecture to those preparing for examinations, perhaps twice a week. The French Revolution was set for examination. Acton was deeply read on the subject and decided to lecture about it.

To his first lecture (ordinary lecture, not the inaugural) came a full room with two or three undergraduates standing and the Master of Trinity standing and his little wife who opened a book to take notes and Miss Gladstone from Newnham who brought along thirty-two of her girls. Dr Gwatkin afterwards came along to say that there were complaints, that Acton talked too fast and they could not take it all in and they could not always catch the proper names; so for this third lecture, still a full room with three or four standing, and with Lord Kelvin the eminent scientist in the audience, and with the wife of the Master of Trinity still taking down every word in her large notebook, he went more slowly and took trouble about the names and watched the many scribbling pens. One of the girls was evidently bowled over because she came afterwards and said that she felt as if she had read twenty volumes; and Lord Kelvin came up and grasped his hand and said it was the best lecture he ever heard and that he never so much regretted the end of the hour. Acton liked praise, but he specially liked praise from people he admired and he admired Kelvin very much.

He wrote to his daughter Annie about it:

> We are not made angry by foolish criticism, and I have less right to [sic] than others. Think how unsympathetic my teaching must be to the philistine, the sordid, the technical, the faddist, the coward, the man of prejudice and passion, the zealot etc. This makes much more than half the world. So I am always surprised at praise, and only wonder at blame, and specially misinterpretation in particular places.[10]

---

[10] Acton to Annie, no. 111.

His next lecture that term was on 8 November and at the end when he talked of Marie Antoinette, he reported that there were old dons who hid their faces in their hands and shook with sobbing[11] and that some in the town were reported to say that it was the finest thing they ever heard. The Newnham girls were still puzzled over his inaugural and petitioned to be allowed a meeting to discuss it with him.

These lectures were delivered once a week at 12:15. He always lectured in one of the lecture rooms in Trinity—fee for persons not members of the university, 1 guinea to be paid at Deighton Bell's. He wrote the lectures out in his beautiful hand and was said by a close colleague Figgis to have delivered them as they were written. Internal evidence suggests that this cannot be true; for sometimes they are not long enough to fill the time for a lecture and the lecturer must have taken room to expand off the cuff; and occasionally a sentence is so incomprehensible that it can only be a note to remind the lecturer to expand it orally. He did not make life easy for himself because he could not quite repeat the same lectures next year, so he had to go on worrying at the text and amending. It was a time of exceptionally hard work. "I accept no invitations to London, and neglect many duties graver than that. It is impossible for me to undertake any writing for a long time to come. I should fail, and it would make me nervous and uncomfortable."[12] The cards in the Cambridge University Library show the labour that lay behind the lectures. He never took a secondary source for granted but sought to track it down to its original. He did not take pleasure in the delivery of the lectures for he disliked public speaking.

Each lecture day at 5 he would be in his rooms in college to give advice to students.

Some who came to pass an examination went away. But others were rivetted. The man was intense about history, at times passionate; it was not a mouth that was talking but a whole being; one hearer calls it, meaning it as a compliment, "an emotional performance." A rational university will hardly appoint as the most junior assistant lecturer someone whose lecture is an emotional performance. The same hearer says that the lecture was "a wonderful work of art" and

---

[11] Acton to Annie, no. 113.

[12] Acton to Henry Sidgwick, 7 November 1895, Trinity College MSS.

leaves pedestrians to worry about the secret of turning a lecture about the past into a wonderful work of art.[13]

The man was felt to be, at the time, and we feel him to be now, altogether bigger than the lectures. Behind the lectures lay a coherent intelligence, rich and varied, struggling with truth and of a total integrity.

It is a question whether people should leave behind them when they die the manuscript of their old lectures. During Acton's lifetime not only the Cambridge Press but other publishers both English and American asked for permission to have his lectures to print and Acton refused. Figgis and Laurence published both sets—1907 and 1910—though the editors were clear about the defects in them for published purposes. Why did they publish? Because they revered the man—because he had grown even more controversial since his death and they wanted to show him as he was—because they thought that for all the oddity of the lectures they contained serious thinking on bits of modern history—and because they were not difficult to publish since Acton wrote them out in a long hand which was easy to read.

The lectures on the French Revolution have this oddness that they begin with two chapters on the background of thought and then the rest of the chapters are a detailed narrative of what happened 1789–94.

He spoke epigrams and aphorisms which were rather halftruths than truths but are powerful on the reader—the earth belongs to those who walk on it, not to those who are underneath (*LFR* 33); It is a grave miscalculation to think that a regular army is stronger than an undisciplined mob (*LFR* 66); the army which gave liberty to France was largely composed of assassins (*LFR* 90); the single page of print (that is the Declaration of the Rights of Man) is stronger than all the armies of Napoleon (*LFR* 107).

Undergraduates reading history were taught that history should be dry, unemotional. Acton held that this was what Ranke, whom he so much admired, had taught us that history ought to be. Teachers used to say, *Never use a superlative*. Acton approved this idea of dryness but did not practise it. He spattered superlatives—the greatest scene in modern history (*LFR* 53), Mirabeau was the best debater in French Parliamentary history (*LFR* 53), Talleyrand was to be feared, and hated

---

[13] John Pollock, *Independent Review*, 2 (April 1904), 366.

and admired, as the most sagacious politician in the world (*LFR* 69); 9th Thermidor is "the most auspicious date in modern history" (*LFR* 284). "There is no record of a finer act of fortitude in all parliamentary history" (it is the personal attack by Cambon on Robespierre, *LFR* 294); "the most brilliant figure on the battlefield of Europe" this is Murat (*LFR* 344). At times the superlatives are allusive and mysterious—the most celebrated of all the Guelphic writers (= Thomas Aquinas), the ablest writer of the Ghibelline party (= Marsilius), "the most brilliant agitator among the continental Socialists," "the most illustrious of the early philosophers" (= Pythagoras), "the wisest man to be found in Athens" (= Solon), the most distinguished English writer of the twelfth century (John of Salisbury), the most learned of Anglican prelates (Ussher), the ablest of the French prelates (Bossuet), the ablest ruler that ever sprung from a revolution (Cromwell), the most popular of bishops (Fénelon), the purest Conservative intellect (Niebuhr), the most intelligent of Greek tyrants (Periander), the greatest theologian of his age (Gerson), the most famous royalist of the Restoration (Chateaubriand), the ablest of historic men (Napoleon); no tyrant "ever used his power to inflict greater suffering or greater wrong" than King Louis XIV. These superlatives showed the same habit of mind which made him choose a list of "the hundred best books."

He had a genius as an anthologist or selector of the telling quotation and putting it onto his card index. He had a fascination about the odd details of history—how the King of France snored more loudly when he was bored by the discussion than when he was asleep (*LFR* 43); how after Charlotte Corday murdered Marat in his bath they went to her room and found the Bible lying open at the story of Judith (*LFR* 265). He loved extraordinary moments and extraordinary careers. Sometimes if a thing was extraordinary he was inclined to believe it. We do not know how the decibels of the King of France's snoring could be tested. On the evidence it is extremely unlikely that they found the Bible open in Charlotte Corday's room, they are far more likely to have found the story of Brutus murdering Caesar, for she really did admire Brutus; but there is no reliable evidence that they found anything of the sort.[14] Such anecdotes explain why there were persons in Cambridge who criticized Acton as a historian whose qualities combined being a Dictionary of Dates and taking pleasure in scandalous stories.[15]

Sometimes there was grim humour. Collot and Fouché were united in sacred bands of friendship—notice Acton's word sacred in the band of friendship. Why were they friends? Because they had joined in putting 1,682 persons to death at Lyons (*LFR* 289). One of Acton's friends said that he concealed much beneath "a grave irony."[16]

He could communicate a sense of the immediacy of history. If you have lived through the Second World War it is hard to realize that for most of the people you talk to it is as remote as the siege of Troy—except for the few who have lost a father or mother or uncle or aunt in it and except (a large exception) for those who belong to a people, like the Jews and the Poles, who suffered tragedy. Acton could tell stories which easily bridged this gap in human memory. The procession of the States-General at Versailles on 5 May 1789 being cheered by the crown, a turning-point in European history, what did it feel like at the time? Acton had relatives who watched the cheering of the new liberal Pope in 1846. An Italian lady did not cheer. They asked her why. She said "Because I was at Versailles in 1789" (*LFR* 55). The anecdote bridged the decades, everyone felt at once how short is time. Acton had a gut-feeling how these actions of the past affect us now—the debate on 8 July 1789 which led to the fall of the Bastille—and, he says, the face of the world was changed, and "the imperishable effects of which will be felt by everyone of us, to the last day of his life" (*LFR* 83). He treasured these moments which linked him to the past. When he went to work in the archives of Venice in 1864 he was presented to the Signora Inocenigo; and it mattered to him that she had in earlier days rented her house to Lord Byron, and it mattered even more to him that as a girl she had

---

[14] The reviewer in *English Historical Review* was critical that Acton should accept a story that Danton offered a bribe to Pitt to save the King's life in return for a large British bribe.

[15] Reported by Maitland, 19 October 1902, Maitland's *Letters*, ed. Fifoot, p. 317.

[16] R. Lane Poole, in *English Historical Review* (October 1902), 696.

danced with the last Doge of Venice,[17] and he loved to tell the historians of Cambridge about this strange link with a vanished world.

Colourless? He had the sense that history is a drama. His account of the flight of the French king and queen to Varennes, and their pursuit and arrest, is narrative history in the most gripping form; we do not wonder that George Macaulay Trevelyan was one of his best pupils.

He was sure that reading history makes a difference to one's person; he said once that there are two books which can make an epoch in a person's life—they are Michelet and Taine—that is the glorifying and the demolishing histories of the French Revolution—and this is even though the books are not good books in his opinion; for example he regarded Taine not as a historian but as a pathologist (*LFR* 370). He can hate historians; and as was predictable of a Whig lord like this, the most hated of all the historians was Carlyle.

And the moral sense kept coming through. Was it bad, all that murder in the Terror? Yes it was very bad, it was murder. But—murder goes on most of the time in other ages—murder is not peculiar to any one country or time or opinion; and if it wins then historians come along and praise it—"the strong man with the dagger is followed by the weaker man with the sponge. First, the criminal who slays; then the sophist who defends the slayer" (*LFR* 92)—historians are nearly as bad as the assassins. If you are an honest historian you prove that everyone is bad—and his last words of advice to his audience in his lectures on the French Revolution, try to deal evenly with friend and foe—but is it possible for an honest historian to have a friend? (*LFR* 373) He solemnly told his hearers to take as a principle of their work, *Never be surprised at the crumbling of an idol or the disclosure of a skeleton.*

The lectures were not so very suitable for undergraduates wishing to pass examinations. Figgis said about them that they "were not so much a mine of instruction as a revelation of the speaker's personality."[18] Gooch, though now he lived in London, came up to attend them and loved them. George Trevelyan attended them and there was quite a sprinkling of senior members of the university. Oscar Browning attended them regularly and said that there were

---

[17] *Lord Acton: The Decisive Decade. 1864–74*, ed. Damian McElrath et al. (Louvain, 1970), p. 129.

[18] Preface to Acton's *LMH*, p. xi.

not many (male) undergraduates, it was a big audience but a lot of them were townsfolk and the lectures could be understood only by those well qualified in the subject;[19] but we should take this with a pinch of salt for Browning afterwards liked to portray himself as the person who taught nitty-gritty history while Acton was the person whose lesser function was only to inspire. Undergraduates were certainly in the audience. E. M. Forster the future novelist attended the lectures and wrote down in his *Commonplace Book* (1885), slightly wrong, that striking sentence "Every villain is followed by a sophist with a sponge"; where the misquotation is kinder to the historians than was Acton's actual text.

The lectures at Cambridge were said by good judges to be "a very good success."[20] The delivery was powerful—a solemn dignity, as though this thing called history is a sacred subject, a quest for what is true and truth is the greatest thing in the world, and this truth is bound up with the moral nature of humanity.

Everything is so exciting—the archives are open at last, the libraries are open—the State Record offices, the Vatican Archives—we can get authentic history and not what people think happened and not what interested parties wish us to think happened—he felt it to be a seed-time for a much truer history than had ever been written in the past. It is exciting because at last we are getting history out of the biases that restricted it—the bias of race and the bias of religion and the bias of nationalism and the State. Now at last we can write a history of the Battle of Waterloo that French and English will both accept or a history of the Reformation which Catholics and Protestants will both see to be fair. Truth is above the propaganda and the biases. It is beginning to be reachable. And reachable by the ordinary reading person. We are about to make history independent of the historians.

"These things are extra territorial, having their home in the sky, and no more confined to race or frontier, than a rainbow or a storm" (letter to Syndics, October 1896)—there speaks the poet of history. To us this is naiveté—in 1995 a Bosnian historian spoke of the history of Bosnia and it was passionate and during it some of the hearers imagined a Serb historian describing the same events. History is easily

---

[19] Oscar Browning, *Memories of Later Years* (1923), p. 17.

[20] Balfour in M. Grant Duff, *Notes from a Diary* (1905), I, p. 20.

turned into propaganda. Hugh Trevor-Roper gave a lecture on German historians and frightened the audience for he forecast what British historians would all be saying now if Hitler had conquered Britain. Acton thought that we had climbed out of nationalism in history. He sang its ideals like a minstrel and the song had beauty and was blind to reality.

Acton was not a pure partisan—he had rigid principles about conscience and liberty—and never concealed evidence that told against him; he never failed to note down the exceptions which spoke against his argument. The contradiction or wonder in the mind, is that he was always yearning, and can be felt to be yearning, to overcome such things as prejudices and see things as they really were.

Human beings are worse in reality than in their reputations. The people we meet look good because we only see the envelope. But the historian is going to read the letters they wrote and what others report that they did. Readers of Acton's pessimistic view of humanity, and the historian's part in it, realize that to have a biography is one of the worst fates that can afflict a suffering person. About individuals in history he could be depressing. He wrote to the Master of Trinity, H. M. Butler: "We must always expect our pupils to see, more and more clearly, that the great men of history were not good men. There is no remedy. One can only strive to pick up every striking, or elevating, or edifying fact, and fix it on their minds."[21] It was a curious contrast, that he held the loftiest ideal about what history could do for human beings, but one of the things it does for them is to depress them about each other. He could dismiss eminent persons with an abusive word: Nelson, "infamous man"; Bismarck, "a great man, and a great scoundrel."

Two pupils who attended his lectures, and were taught by him privately, left their impressions of him as a teacher. These are valuable because most judgements of him came from posterity, those who did not know him and judged him by the posthumous print which he did not mean to publish; through which various adverse judge-

---

[21] Acton to H. M. Butler, CUL Add. MSS 7339/3.

ments were recorded—that he so loved lists of books that he was less a historian than a bibliographer; that despite his own advice he failed to doubt the evidence enough and hence was too dogmatic; that he was like a mausoleum, impressive to look at but not a guide to the living; that he made history too majestic.

The two pupils took very different views of him. George Trevelyan was not sure. Acton had been doubtful about Trevelyan—in the first encounters he was an enthusiast for this able pupil but when Trevelyan began to write immaturely Acton thought that the work was not as good as he had expected it to be and ought to have been better. Trevelyan reciprocated doubt about Acton. The lectures were delivered, he said, as though the speaker was an oracle. This was a sage talking, who had travelled thither from the antique lands of European statecraft, "with the brow of Plato above the reserved and epigrammatic lips of the diplomatist." There is an implied doubt in the sentence. Trevelyan thought afterwards that he would not have been remembered as a historian but for the other qualities which were not historical. But he confessed that Acton helped to make the history school great, especially because he made it respected in the university.

The second pupil whose record we have expressed a very different and more uninhibited opinion. During the years when Acton was at Cambridge the great lawyer Sir Frederick Pollock, himself a former fellow of Trinity Cambridge, was the professor of jurisprudence at Oxford. He sent his son John to Trinity after him. John arrived and read history and found Acton his professor and in his own college. The result was more like reverence than admiration; for a unique person, the biggest historian of them all, not only without parallel in his learning perhaps, but familiar with Western literature, a man of wit and passion, "with the power to tear the heart from many mysteries," a citizen of the world by birth, without prejudice or fear, "with a burning zeal for the cause of truth and the triumph of justice." He carried all this weight of learning with ease and without being heavy—"one of the richest of human minds." Acton evidently lent him books, and even his copies of manuscripts. But Pollock found each lecture an experience. "Never before had a young man come into the presence of such intensity of conviction as was sounded by

21

every word" and it was this which gave the lectures "their amazing force and vitality."[22]

THE ORGANIZATION OF HISTORY

While he was on the History Board, the Tripos was divided like other Triposes into two parts. He did not speak much at meetings and he approved rather than led what was done. But he had more weight behind the scenes than this suggests. He regarded the plan for reform of the syllabus as his own and was pleased that when it was debated the members of the Theological Faculty came to stand on his side because they regarded him as the lay defender of religion in the university and thought that religion was helped by his historical scheme. He refused to accept a proposal that he should become chairman of the History Board. According to Browning's memory, he refused this more than once and Browning thought that it was his duty to accept. Maitland once wrote a despairing cry: "The History Board consumes endless time ... At present Acton = 0. I wish he would bless or curse or do something."[23] Once when he was out of the room they took the moment to elect him chairman when he could not protest but after he came back he persuaded them that it was not right that he should be made to serve.

He made a friend for ever over the chairmanship. Gwatkin the professor of church history looked odd and sounded odder, and was a militant Protestant. The board was resolute not to have Gwatkin as its chairman. Acton resented what he called their "dead set" against Gwatkin, and the Catholic professor proposed Gwatkin for chairman and carried the motion because they did not like to oppose Acton. It is not probable that the resulting chairmanship was always effective; but thenceforth Gwatkin was dedicated to Acton.

The number of students rose steadily: 1897, 48; 1898, 54; 1899, 106; 1900, 98; 1901, 114; 1902, 129—nearly three times during those last six years of his life.

---

[22] Trevelyan, *Autobiography* (1949), p. 17; *Clio a Muse*, pp. 177ff, especially 183; John Pollock, *Independent Review* (April 1904).

[23] Maitland's *Letters*, ed. Fifoot, p. 177.

THE PUPILS

It hurt him when he came to Cambridge that some of the best scholars in the university regarded history as a second-class subject. If you had a brain you read classics, if you had not you did history or science. That was not just pain, it offended him deeply, he felt it almost as though it was an insult to himself. Figgis thought that Acton was the man who did more than anyone to remove this stain and persuade the scholars that this is a subject which elicits high qualities of the mind and is of fundamental importance to the human race. George Trevelyan agreed. This was what Acton achieved.

When inquirers had a private conversation with Acton about history they felt that the wisdom of the ages was speaking through him; and this came over nearly as powerfully in lectures, except that the wisdom of the ages was cluttered up by historical facts. In a sense Acton was the poet of history. History, he says, is to be "not a burden on the memory but an illumination of the soul."[24]

With individual pupils he was excellent, really interested in them, sending them piles of books they had never heard of in languages which they did not know how to translate and with a letter telling them this was only the first batch and that more would follow later. This was almost an obsession with him; he loved lists of books and here was a chance to show people that the list really existed. He was never bored by people who came to ask him questions; he liked questions and never made the questioner feel a fool or an ignoramus. He was patient, accessible, and inspiring in encouragement. He asked them questions, really wanting to know what they thought and perhaps to learn from them.

He could be quite fierce in his reports. Here is a report on one student: "It would do him good to devote a year to the reign of Antiochus, or the policy of Lysander, or something remoter still, that he may learn to put proof in the place of assertion, and to sit tight on the safety valve of opinion." He could be "cruel" at need. One showy, insubstantial essay was abused eloquently. Pollock recorded an experience of an undergraduate who must have been himself. He

---

[24] Report to Syndics of Cambridge University Press, reprinted in *The Cambridge Modern History* (1907), p. 20.

read Fouché's Memoirs, recently translated into English, and used them to write an essay on Austrian policy in the year of Waterloo, but did not mention where he found his facts. When he read the essay to Acton, he received high praise for it, and then a few light corrections; and suddenly at the end Acton said, "I think you made some use of Fouché's Memoirs. I suppose you know they are not authentic." This was not the only time when Acton devastated a pupil. But history is difficult. The undergraduate need not have been so squashed. Fouché's Memoirs were published soon after his death and his family went to court to prove them a forgery and won from the courts the destruction of all copies. All through the nineteenth century they were believed to be a fabrication and were still so believed when Acton listened to Pollock's essay. But at that very moment opinion among historians began to turn to the conviction that total fabrication was impossible and that many pages of them were written by Fouché himself.

Acton asked Oscar Browning to tell his students that he was not formidable as they might think—"I am a comparatively domesticated animal, and not so wild a beast as I look."[25]

Some of Acton's pupils made big contributions to history later. They did it in Actonian ways.

R. V. Laurence, whom Acton called "my special pupil," wrote nothing, like his master. Figgis, whom he described as a tutor who has particularly "attached himself to me" and who helped him with an affectionate care as he moved towards illness, was brilliant on Church and State (which was one of his greatest interests); Gutteridge made a difference not to history but to international law and Acton thought the training of international lawyers a part of the business of teaching history; Trevelyan contributed in an original way to Italian history as well as English; Gooch was a Germanic polymath like Acton; Clapham made advances in economic history; Temperley applied international law to the making of treaties; and Benians took history out of Europe and across the world.

---

[25] Acton to Browning, 3 and 22 March 1896, Browning MSS, King's College.

Acton founded the Trinity College Historical Society which still goes on. As a Trinity College Historical Society it had this peculiarity that the members did not need to belong to Trinity—Maitland, Acton's close friend and colleague, professor at Downing College and also of Trinity, was a founder member—but only the members of Trinity had votes, so early on there was a charming mock seventeenth-century petition from the historian Figgis "from my poor garret, starving for lack of two shillings," who was Fellow of St Catharine's and a member, that this was *taxation without representation* because the subscription was put up from one shilling a year to two shillings a year without him having any say in this tax.

The first volume of the minutes of the Society is in the Wren Library and is fun. Trevelyan was one of the original members, so was Cunningham the founder of economic history in Cambridge, and Maitland. Four other future professors were elected members in the next few meetings and Figgis would have made a fifth if he had not been torpedoed by a submarine. One of the members, outrageously unActonian in his attitudes to history, was Lytton Strachey; but the minutes show that he was an infrequent attender; and perhaps we may think that it was not that he was unActonian because he was an infrequent attender but an infrequent attender because he was unActonian. But—was he altogether unActonian? In Strachey one of the axioms of Acton was carried to excess, even corrupted. The doctrine that conditioned Lytton Strachey's work was this, men and women are worse than their public reputations. Let us then enjoy demolishing those reputations. The difference, unspoken, was this: Acton had a faith that however bad we all are, there is a moral nature in the world which enables us slowly, by fits and starts, to make it less bad. Strachey had no such faith. We are bad and what happens to the world is just what you would expect as a result.

POLITICAL RIGHT

Inside his lecturing was his ethics of politics.

Politics mean compromise. In politics we need to choose the less bad course because it is a practicable course and we cannot achieve a better. Moral right means no compromise; we have to decide for the right and let the practicable take care of itself. This tension between

25

sane political practice and any sound political ideal continually concerned him. He worried over the truth in the saying of the old Greek philosopher Chrysippus that in politics it is impossible to please both gods and men at the same time.

History is the conscience of the human race—these exploiters and murderers die prosperous but they cannot for ever escape because history tells what they were like.

States when they are in crisis demand more power at the centre and the appetite grows until they create absolutist regimes or police States. The most famous quotation from Acton has always been the single sentence, "*Power tends to corrupt; and absolute power corrupts absolutely.*" This was not a passing *mot*, it expressed everything about history that he felt passionately. "The possession of unlimited power corrodes the conscience, hardens the heart, and confounds the understanding."

He held that any government by the purest form of democracy—that is direct election by all the people to a single assembly which has sovereign power—was sure to end in tyranny and therefore democracies need self-limitation by some form of mixed constitution. He drew this lesson from Athens.

> The lesson of their experience ... teaches that government by the whole people, being the government of the most numerous and most powerful class, is an evil of the same nature as an unmixed monarchy, and requires, for nearly the same reasons, institutions that shall protect it against itself, and shall uphold the permanent reign of law against arbitrary revolutions of opinion.

A unanimous meeting of ordinary people is capable of deciding what is wholly wrong or wholly immoral. Therefore there is a standard of right for the ultimate mood of a people which does not depend upon the unanimity of the voters, far less on the majority of the voters. The obvious problem here Acton did not attempt to solve—that consciences can be almost as misled as votes.

His third principle was the supreme value of the individual. All States want to make, as he said, "the passengers exist for the sake of the ship," "they prefer the ship to the crew." All governments if they are to survive must content a majority of the people; and it is easier to make the people happy if government takes less notice of the rights of the minority of the people. Writers had argued that like ancient Athens modern democracy could not exist without being supplemented by a form of slavery; for the particular difficulty of democracy was its tendency to end in a Communism which Acton regarded as a system which rode over the rights of the individual; since the individuals could never preserve their private right and their private freedom unless they were allowed the possession of property. "A people averse to the institution of private property is without the first element of freedom."

In his eyes the law of human rights—which was not a phrase he liked to use—was a necessity to any moral form of state. He regarded the general acceptance of moral principles as a necessity if the democracy was to survive. Freedom cannot exist for long in a State unless most of the people have an agreement on moral principles and accept the State as more than a mere instrument for protecting them against enemies or criminals or for promoting their prosperity by a centralized management of money and trade and communications.

This preference for democratic regimes with a mixed constitution was not based upon his early experience of the United States. He travelled to the United States during 1853 and was rather contemptuous of what he found. Five years later he was still unhappy with the constitution of the United States and thought it as defective as the Russian—the Russian system too absolute to be good government and the American system too popular to be good government. But in his maturity he looked back upon the American revolution as the beginning of a new epoch in the history of the world. All previous attempts at democracy ended in some form of tyranny by a majority over minorities. But this, he thought, was a democracy which set limits to the authority even of the sovereign people and succeeded in preserving the rights of minorities. It had carried into the world two ideas which old Europe had found it very hard to accept: first, that a revolution may be an act of justice and help to create justice; and second, that a constitution which tries to give "rule" to the people, and which had always been regarded as an unsafe form of constitution because it meant putting power into the hands of ignorant or bribable voters, could under certain conditions be a safe way for a State to be organized without losing its effectiveness or its justice as a government. He came in the end to feel that the American constitution was "the grandest polity in the history of mankind."

He always saw how fragile a possession is liberty—"the delicate fruit of a mature civilization." He was also aware how many enemies it had. States need to go to war—and warring States cannot be free. Illiterate peoples cannot be free because they are at the mercy of propaganda and their superstition will not allow others to be free; as religious majorities in the world still persecute or restrain religious minorities. A starving people will not be free because it needs bread far more than liberty and will care nothing for liberty until it has food. And freedom has lesser enemies in individuals who want power and see the chance of it by control of an army or a police.

Is absolute power sometimes better? Especially in crises? He had a hereditary reason to believe that it might be. In the Bourbon kingdom of Naples his grandfather was a successful prime minister. The King's attitude was that this is a poor and suffering people without enough education yet to contribute to politics. Give them democratic institutions and you create strife and probably murder in the society. It will be far better to keep power, give them a good administration, maintain public order, do all that can be done to diminish their suffering and their poverty, and develop the schools to educate them. Acton could portray the theory of absolutism in all its plausibility and knew that in the corruptions of humanity this method was an illusion and could not work. One wonders what he would have said at the doctrine of the generals in the Algeria or Turkey of our day that if you give the power to an illiterate and fundamentalist society the immediate result is tyranny and all the women thrust back under veils and male oppression. For despite this hereditary reason for thinking that there are cases where absolute power is best, he did not believe it at all. He was sure that no king nor queen nor dictator has the right to rule without the consent of the people and that the people may depose such rulers, even after they came to power by legitimate means, if they turn their power over the people into a tyranny.

This faith in liberty was a basis of Acton's power in the intellectual generation that came after him, even or especially in the generation which astonished itself by meeting Fascists and Nazis when it expected to meet government by the people for the people. He made liberty not just a political expedient but a moral right; and he had a mystical sense that this moral right would slowly conquer the world.

He hated every form of oppression; a class of warriors trampling on the weak; a class of rich grinding down the poor; a class of educated elite exploiting the illiterate. He knew that if we want government by the "best people" in the State, we can never identify *best* with all the educated or all the property-owners or all the persons with political experience. Some people in the "uneducated class" will be more responsible in their attitude to the State than some of the educated. Some of the poor will be better at seeking good government than some of the rich because good government might need to tread on the interests of the rich.

This hatred of oppression and corruption keeps coming through in Acton's prose. He was conscious of the danger of a class war and the need to protect the weaker against it. He was sure that experience proved that no single person is to be trusted with power over others. But he was painfully aware of the enigma, how, if you cannot trust any one person with power, you will be able to trust twenty? Or a million? He saw, whether he surveyed the ancient or his contemporary world, famous political philosophers advocating doctrines that were criminal and absurd.

And yet he was a student who wondered at the achievements of humanity. This was another source of his influence. He saw corruption and slavery and crime: and yet could exult in what whole societies had achieved. He could think Socialism or Communism mistaken because they wanted to do without private property which was a necessity for a free society. Yet he could see why they attracted. He could see the weakness and the superstitions of Churches and the exploitation by churchmen and yet be sure that Judaism and Christianity contributed vastly to the development of civilization and the ideas of liberty. He could see ancient Greek tyranny or mob rule or slave society for what it was and yet talk of the generation of those who succeeded Pericles in Athens as those "whose works, in poetry and eloquence, are still the envy of the world, and in history, philosophy and politics remain unsurpassed." He could see that despite the corruptions there was "a noble literature," "a priceless treasure of political knowledge."

Without having any theory of "great men" in history, he could yet feel this admiration for individuals: for a Pericles himself or a Plato.

He expected that federations were fertile in the civilizing process because if two or more peoples lived within a single umbrella-State the gifts of each race and culture would affect the other races and cultures and there would be a healthy development of the whole society. "It is in the cauldron of the State that the fusion takes place by which the vigour, the knowledge, and the capacity of one portion of mankind may be communicated to another." He thought Britain and Switzerland were blessed in this way. He preferred Austro-Hungary to national states in Croatia or Serbia or Bohemia or Slovakia. He would have encouraged the drive in the nineteen-nineties towards forms of federalism in Europe. But when a lady pupil said to him that petty tyranny occurred in small States, he was rude to her: "that is the silly thing that vulgar people say."[26]

He was convinced that the freedom of the press is a necessity for the development of freedom of the citizen and he had no conception of the possibility that the freedom of the press could be abused.

He was convinced that since the conscience is the heart of the quest for liberty, the religious conscience is the ultimate source of that quest; he used the evidence of the post-Reformation struggles after toleration as the historical proof of this belief; and therefore he was assured that the place of religion in the State is of the first importance to those who wish for a free society. "Religious liberty is the generating principle of civil liberty, and civil liberty is the necessary condition of religious liberty."

The presence of Acton in Cambridge confronted his Church with a difficulty. Here was a Catholic who now had a public post in the non-Catholic world. It was better if that were used by the Church. But this Catholic was regarded by many Catholics as anti-Catholic—if he still stood by his old opinions.

The parish priest at Cambridge was bothered by the coming of a heretic. By his own confession, he was deeply prejudiced against Acton. He was anxious how to behave to an alleged Catholic who had just been elected a professor amid maximum publicity.

---

[26] Pollock, p. 377.

He consulted the Archbishop of Westminster. Cardinal Herbert Vaughan had already acted. As soon as Acton's chair was announced he wrote to him to congratulate him and to say that he felt confident "in your goodness and fidelity to the Church."

> I know and understand something of the awful trials you must have gone through in the years past, and I cannot but thank God that you are what I believe you to be—faithful and loyal to God and His Church, though perhaps by your great learning and knowledge of the human—in this same Church—tried beyond other men.

And Vaughan signed it: "Your faithful and devoted servant."

It is obvious that Acton was very much moved by this letter. After a quarter of a century of suspicion and coldness from the hierarchy (which he had done almost everything possible to deserve) he found that on being elected to a Cambridge professorship he was not only a forgiven man but forgiven in generous language. He evidently did not know how to reply at first, for although he was down with a congestion of the lungs when the cardinal's letter arrived, he was able to write other letters during the next six weeks in which he failed to reply to the cardinal.

When at last he replied (20 April 1895) he wholeheartedly accepted the olive-branch:

> ... I received from your Eminence the kindest and most consoling letter that it has ever been my happy fortune to possess. If I was not afraid of being presumptuous I would in reply assure you that you have judged me rightly as well as most graciously, and I beg that you will believe in my sincere gratitude for all you say.... My Cambridge office is full of interest and promising opportunities; but the danger is that it is almost more a platform before the country than a Cathedra with serious students under it.

And Acton signed himself: "your Eminence's most faithful and obedient servant."[27]

---

[27] Westminster Archives, V/1/13/8; my thanks to the archivist Miss Poyser, Cf. Snead-Cox, *Life of Cardinal Vaughan* (1910), II, pp. 298-9.

On 5 July 1895 Acton even lunched with the Cardinal, who was "as pleasant as he always is."[28]

Thus Acton had been put, so to speak, into a state of grace with his Church without any need to recant, or profess anything which he could not profess, or make any declaration about the sense in which he accepted or put up with the Vatican decrees. The hesitation about the reply could only be because he must have wondered whether in accepting the olive-branch he was necessarily giving the cardinal the impression that he was a more conventional Catholic than he was and whether he had a duty of honesty to say so. Vaughan had said that he believed him to be faithful and loyal to God and his Church. That was just what Acton believed himself to be. On reflection he felt no duty to explain in detail to Vaughan that they were likely to hold different opinions on what the faith of a faithful and loyal Catholic ought to be; for Vaughan had shown no disposition to enquire. When the parish priest at Cambridge consulted Vaughan how he was to treat this formidable and heretical figure, Vaughan showed him Acton's letter and told him to treat Acton as one of the faithful. Hence the parish priest invited Acton to carry the canopy over the host in procession, and Acton accepted—coming in academical dress. Hence Vaughan invited Acton to attend the laying of the foundation stone of Westminster Cathedral and to speak at the luncheon afterwards; which invitation also Acton accepted. It was as important to him to be seen to be a Catholic as not to have to retract. It was the scholarly Jesuit Father Herbert Thurston who was to point out, eleven years later, that Acton had retracted nothing. Yet Acton did tell the parish priest, according to that priest's testimony, that he could now look back upon his trials as on "a hideous nightmare from which the glory and peace of waking has been intense."

THE CAMBRIDGE MODERN HISTORY

The historians have said that Acton did not invent the idea of the Cambridge histories; it was invented by the Press Syndicate of 1896 and put to Acton who turned it into a possible reality. The archives confirm that statement. But the archives also show that the Syndics

---

[28] Acton to Annie, no. 108, 5 July 1895.

thought of the idea early that year because the presence of Acton in Cambridge had put it into their heads. If Acton had not been there to consult and approach, they would not have proceeded in this form. They had a professor who believed in a universal history and that made them willing to believe in it themselves.

There was a minority on the committee and a majority. The leader of the minority was the classical scholar Leonard Whibley, who did not think the plan practicable. The majority who thought that the plan was practicable provided, and only provided, that Acton led it, were the two most eminent scholars in the room: Maitland and Henry Jackson. Maitland was very important to the plan, and to Acton. He was the historian on the Syndicate who had an absolute confidence about both the plan and its editor. He was also the person on the Syndicate who gave Acton the confidence of feeling that the Syndicate would understand what he was at.

The Syndics had the idea of a history of the world. They kept calling it a Universal History. In discussion with Acton they removed all the world before the Renaissance with the possibility of doing the world before the Renaissance later. But in their minutes they still referred to it for the next three years as the Universal History. Six months before they announced it they provisionally invited Acton to edit it. On 21 May 1896 he wrote the secretary a reply saying yes. "I have not hesitated as much as I ought to do, on account of the difficulty, because my office here makes it a duty not to be declined, and because such an opportunity of promoting his own ideas for the treatment of history has seldom been given to any man."

This shows that he was aware of something of what lay ahead. He was not aware how much lay ahead or of how the project was to bring him to his grave.

The plan was announced in *The Times* and *The Athenaeum* on 12 December 1896.

Acton chose the authors. It was not a sinecure. He wrote in his own hand letters consulting people about authors, to authors themselves whom he trusted, second or third efforts at authors who refused, letters to find out whether a proposed author knew the necessary European languages well enough, or to find out whether someone who had done nothing but write about wee moments of history would be capable of a general sweep of history; thinking whether the balance was right, economic or constitutional or the realm of thought and art; arguing whether it was better to choose a famous person who would be offended if you tried to edit his work, or a young person who would do just what you wanted if you edited the text; interviewing those in difficulty in his rooms in Nevile's Court or at the Athenaeum in London; deciding whether if someone did not answer his letters he was refusing or whether he was still thinking about it.

He was amazingly lucky. Because nothing like this had happened before, the proposed authors were interested to take part and many felt honoured that they should be chosen by Acton. Authors might accept the work and then die on him.[29] The loss of Hodgkin they felt very serious (a refusal not a death). Acton was pained at the refusals. Maitland said to Jackson, "Why does not his omniscient lordship write the whole of the book? He could do it and come up smiling." Some people applied to take part—Oscar Browning among the first—though his application was very frank, "I sleep badly and can scarcely read a book."[30] Acton realised that for local political reasons he must use Browning but had a difficulty thinking of a subject which he could safely entrust to that author; and finally pitched on the eighteenth century because Acton seemed to be under the illusion that less happened in those decades.

Acton loved lists of the best historians in the world and wanted them all to write. One of the most enjoyable occupations in his whole academic life consisted in producing the names of 120 first-class historians for the Syndics of the Cambridge Press to consider. Acton assumed that if you were a first-class historian you could write about any bit of history. His friends had to discourage him from trying to get a famous medievalist to write about King Frederick the Great. He did sometimes have wild ideas about historians: he had the idea that they might hire Westcott, who was a Platonist and the least historical mind in England—he saw everything as a bit of eternity. Acton had the idea of offering Calvin to Hodgkin, who was a Quaker—and Quakers being even more against Calvin than are Roman Catholics, the result was comic. Someone in St. John's College refused with these words: "I am more than ordinarily ignorant of general history.

---

[29] Maitland's *Letters*, ed. Fifoot, p. 241.

[30] CUL Add. MSS 6443/112.

I have no gift of style, and writing is a longdrawn agony to me ... I have ... no literary power, and no historical bent, much less historical knowledge."[31]

Still, Acton knew a historian when he saw one. His greatest assets were Firth and the reluctant S. R. Gardiner. There are a lot of charming comments on authors among the papers. There were arguments: some thought a historian was good and some did not—the future Cardinal Gasquet was a case in point. Acton finally believed in him and got him to write but the contribution which he produced gave endless trouble to the editors.

There were diplomatic considerations—how you address a person, for instance. Some people who are professors like to be called Professor and others who are professors like to be addressed as Mr. When he compiled the names, the number of Reverends on the list looked too high, so Acton decided to call the economic historian Cunningham Dr. Cunningham and not Archdeacon. Acton kept suggesting Miss Shaw but no one knew who she was. For a time they thought he might be thinking of George Bernard Shaw; but she turned out to be a Miss Nora Shaw who cared about colonial history.

In one way Acton was a marvellous correspondent; he wrote a lot of letters and every letter tells. But he did nothing about letters if he did not know what to do. An American was asked to write. He asked the secretary of the Press to ask Acton to tell him what was wanted. Acton was asked; he did not reply. The American wrote directly to Acton but no reply. The American wrote to the Press begging they push Acton to write.

He was clear about the nature of the enterprise to the secretary of the Press, Richard Wright, 30 May 1897:

> The work is to be plain, and smooth, and clear, giving all that a general-educated reader wants but at the same time so scientific and erudite at the base, and in the materials employed and indicated, as to satisfy scholars and experts. The tone to be strictly scientific in the sense that no national, political or religious proclivity will be exhibited, or offended. In this respect, as in respect of fullness and accuracy, every contribution to be seriously revised and checked.

[31] Foxwell, in CUL Add. MSS 6443/156.

He realised that this would be more difficult than he laid down. "Our danger will be that some men will not readily pocket their private opinions, in politics, religion, and the like—and we must be enabled to chisel all that down."

Soon he knew that he needed help. A. W. Ward was of the family of Arnold of Rugby and being educated partly in Germany was good at European history with a Germanic style. It is remarkable that of the two people who did most to create the first *Cambridge Modern History* one had all his university education in Germany and the other had a lot of his schooling in Germany. The Press soon made Ward an assistant editor. Two years later Ward felt that he was doing most of the work and demanded more pay and the title of co-editor. The Syndicate was willing for a bit more pay but would have nothing to do with any editor except Acton and Ward resigned.

All the part-help did not remove the burden. In 1899–1900 Figgis saw that Acton could do nothing else but think about this History and feared that the labour of it was going to kill him. Maitland and Charlotte Blennerhassett both thought that this work helped bring Acton to his death. He was not a natural administrator. He had taken on the busiest job of editor yet seen and had small qualities as an editor except the quality of knowing a scholar when he saw one. He was a perfectionist and kept correcting people's texts even after they had already gone through more than one draft.

In January 1900 Acton realized that he could not do it and asked that Ward should be a joint editor and that fees to himself should be reduced or abandoned. The Syndics were not going to lose the selling power of Acton's name and refused this outright. Acton asked them, if they would not make Ward a joint editor, would they not make Maitland? They did not even comment on this last proposal. On 31 March 1900 he wrote a depressed letter to Ward saying that the best thing for the Syndics "would be that the Chair of History should soon be vacant."

In April 1901 he suffered a stroke. It was the sort of stroke that brought some paralysis. The Syndicate sent a warm-hearted message of sympathy and good will begging him not to do any more till he was rested and completely recovered. In July 1901 the Syndics received a letter from Acton's son Richard on behalf of his father resigning the editorship.

Among the obituaries, that in *The Times* caused a little disquiet in Cambridge. It said good things and true things: his vast learning, his obscure style, his questionable influence on Gladstone's politics, his lack of feeling for poetry, his brilliance as a conversationalist, in which he equalled Macaulay, his charm and kindness to everyone; but then it said that he was limited by a certain mental timidity, a distinct want of national fibre. "With greater moral courage and a more sturdy literary conscience Lord Acton would have made a more striking mark in letters and in public affairs; but his life, as it was, remains a splendid example of devotion to study, and historical research, and to the cause of truth."

The language made Cambridge doubt. Lack of fibre? Lack of moral courage? Mental timidity? There is in the library of Trinity an unpublished letter from Acton's friend and colleague, Henry Jackson. He wrote it after he read *The Times* obituary.

> I cannot guess who has written it; apparently someone who was well-informed, but not sympathetic either to Acton or to Gladstone. Someone told me a little while ago that Acton would be regarded as Gladstone's evil genius, for that Acton wrote letters about public affairs to Mary Drew, which she was to read to Gladstone when she saw a favourable moment. The last words of the article—"a splendid example of devotion to study, to historical research, and to *the cause of truth*—and especially those which I have underlined, seem to me quite just. But I think that "a certain mental timidity" is a phrase which may mislead. I think he never shrank from the conclusions to which the premises pointed; but he was not a man of action, and I think, in general, left others to carry things into effect.[32]

What the leading historian among his colleagues, Maitland, remembered was not Acton's books of lectures, for Maitland died before any of them was published. Even if he had seen the books, he would have remembered something better still. Acton was a genius not when he wrote history but when he spoke about history. What Maitland

---

[32] Henry Jackson to H. M. Butler, 23 June 1902, Trinity College MSS.

remembered above all were Acton's talks in his home of Chaucer Road on Sunday afternoons. "I shall never forget the few talks that I had with Acton ... in a short time he did an enormous deal to improve the position of history here and I think his loss irreparable."[33]

---

[33] Maitland, *Collected Papers* (Cambridge, 1911), III; obituary of Acton in *Cambridge Review*, 16 October 1902; *Letters*, ed. Fifoot, pp. 37 and 323.

2

FREEDOM OF THOUGHT
AND COMMITMENT TO GOD

Acton's Untimely Impulse for a Liberal Theory*

Johann Christian Koecke

Translated by Victoria Huizinga

L ord Acton's writings are not an easy read. His style is convoluted, and he likes to illustrate his thoughts with historical examples that are unfamiliar to anyone with an average education. In light of this, a work about him should at least provide an easy introduction. Among the people who put their thoughts down on paper there are three types: those whose writings overshadow their lives and personalities; those whose lives overshadow their writing; and those whose lives and writings can only be understood if one interprets each in the light of the other.

Undoubtedly, John Emerich Edward Dalberg Acton belonged to the third group of writers. He was a distinguished aristocrat; scrupulous scholar; lord-in-waiting for her majesty, the Queen of England and Ireland and Empress of India; a member of the House of Lords; as well as an unsuccessful representative of the House of Commons. He was one of the most curious public figures of the nineteenth century, a century that was full of curious figures and that many historians say

---

*Originally published in German as "Freiheit des Geistes und Bindung an Gott. Actons unzeitgemäße Impulse für die liberale Theorie," in *Glaube, Gewissen, Freiheit. Lord Acton und die religiösen Grundlagen der liberalen Gesellschaft*, ed. Christoph Böhr, Philipp W. Hildmann, and Johann Christian Koecke (Wiesbaden: Springer, 2015), 85–98.

lasted until the July Crisis of 1914. Acton was uncharacteristic for his time and combined unique attributes and activities that we generally will have to examine one by one in order not to lose the big picture. One cannot simply start with his "teachings"; instead, one first must engage with what sets him apart from others.

During a time when nations and people groups everywhere in Europe were becoming self-aware, created borders to separate themselves from each other, and achieved unity in states, Lord Acton was busy living an eighteenth-century type of aristocratic cosmopolitanism: He was born in Naples, the son of an English adventurer who worked for the Catholic king of Naples and the Kingdom of the Two Sicilies. His mother, whose maiden name was Dalberg, came from a very influential Catholic family in Rhine Hessia. Her uncle was prince-primate of the Rhenish Confederation, and her father was a close advisor to Talleyrand. This explains why she was raised in Paris and spoke French better than German. After the death of her husband, Acton's father, she married the English aristocrat Lord Granville. As a result of this marriage, Acton became more involved with his family's English homeland. Later he studied with Ignaz von Döllinger in Munich and experienced his academic awakening by studying the German historical-critical method. He married the daughter of the Italian-Bavarian count Arco-Valley and made Lake Tegernsee in Germany his favorite place of residence. Munich, Shropshire, Tegernsee, and Rome—German, English, French, and Italian—he must have thought of nationalism as the shrinkage of the rational mind.

Acton was a peer in the House of Lords. Later in life Acton held the office of lord-in-waiting and was Regius Professor of modern history at Cambridge University—and as a Catholic no less! For the unreflective British consciousness of that time, Catholics were thought of as beefy figures, mainly Irish. Catholics worked in the shipping industry, factories, and mining. They were seen as superstitious folk who attributed an inexplicable and mystical meaning to simple water and wafers. This general attitude toward Catholics explains why Acton studied in Munich rather than in Britain: Cambridge rejected him on the grounds of being a Catholic.

But for Acton, being British and Catholic was not enough incommensurability. He was very different from his Catholic compatriots, who circled the wagons to keep a world in diaspora, marked by a puristic, doctrinaire Catholicism. They also shared a sense of victimization and defensiveness. Acton had no desire for closeness to his British Catholic peers; because of his German, French, and Italian studies and contacts, he was too strongly rooted in the established Catholicism on the Continent. And thus, because of his passionate struggle against both the doctrine of papal infallibility and the decisions of the First Vatican Council, he made enemies out of two groups in particular: the Roman Camarilla and the British Catholic functionary caste.

A Brit, cosmopolitan Catholic, political liberal, and personally deeply religious and pious. In a sense, he was caught in the middle—he found himself between a rock and a hard place. Acton comes from Whiggism. He was a British liberal his entire life and a close advisor of Gladstone. He abhorred the Conservatives' amoral intransigence as well as their snobbery. During his less than successful time in the House of Commons, he worked on plans to improve political ties with Ireland but then transferred his liberalism to the realm of theory and the study of history.

He is classified as a liberal and became an idol for his followers Friedrich August von Hayek and Ludwig von Mises. It is interesting that only the Acton Institute in the United States has named itself after him. Only thinkable in the United States, the Acton Institute's mission is to "promote a free and virtuous society characterized by individual liberty and sustained by religious principles."[1] To the continental Catholic ear this mix of free-market economy, individual liberty, and religious principles sounds like a Trojan horse from Chicago. And yet the name Acton is not entirely unencumbered even for Anglo-Saxon ears. In April 1947, close to Montreux, a gathering of leading liberal economists and philosophers took place under Hayek's leadership, seeking ways to reinvigorate liberalism after the war. When the suggestion was made to name this new society the Acton-Tocqueville Society, it was turned down. A leading representative of the Chicago School, Frank Knight, argued that it would be too much to name a

---

[1] Acton Institute, "About the Acton Institute," http://www.acton.org/about.

liberal society after *two* Roman Catholics. Then the group decided on the less controversial name: Mont Pelerin Society.[2]

Acton may have been a liberal, but he had no interest in economics. Golo Mann quotes an "old lady from Munich" who had this to say: "His pockets were always full of gold coins that he loved to jingle and that he very absent-mindedly and generously spent for others."[3] Acton lost one fortune (his own) by buying books and ordering copies from archives and libraries, so that in the end the magnificent castle that belonged to his maternal family had to be sold to a leather manufacturer. So if he was a political liberal, did that also mean he was a liberal Catholic? What even is a liberal Catholic? Is it a Catholic who is politically liberal, or a Catholic who strives for more liberty and participation inside the church? Or even a Catholic whose religious observance is on the mild side (some would say lukewarm), who is not too concerned about right Catholic doctrine, in other words a representative of the Rhenish blithe spirit?

Acton was at any rate an enigma to many. Politically, he was unequivocally liberal, and personally, he was unequivocally pious. Roland Hill, his biographer, describes him as downright childlike in his piety. Hill quotes Acton as saying, "I am not concious that I ever in my life had the slightest shadow of a doubt about any dogma of the Catholic church."[4] Yet he became a passionate opponent of the doctrine of papal infallibility as it was declared by Pope Pius IX at the First Vatican Council in July 1870. For many Catholics of his time, who made the simple equation that being Catholic equals being loyal to the pope, this was incomprehensible. In order to understand

---

[2] Cf. Erik von Kuehnelt-Leddihn, "The Four Liberalisms," *Religion & Liberty* 2, no. 4 (1992), http://www.acton.org/pub/religion-liberty/volume-2-number-4/four-liberalisms.

[3] Golo Mann, *Lord Acton*, in *Zeiten und Figuren, Schriften aus vier Jahrzehnten* (Frankfurt am Main: Fischer-Taschenbuch-Verlag, 1979), 36ff. (quote on p. 36).

[4] Roland Hill, *Lord Acton* (New Haven: Yale University Press, 2000), 406. Here at the beginning of this essay I have forgone giving biographic details from Hill's research and from reflecting on Golo Mann's prosaic intuition. Both Hill's biography and Mann's essay in a nutshell are rich sources for anyone interested in the writings and life of Acton.

Acton's obsessive opposition here, we must look at his doctrine of two kingdoms. I shall discuss this in more depth later.

Acton and the liberal theory—herein we find at least two questions and themes. Let's start with the less controversial one: Acton and theory. Did Acton have a theory? Did he contribute to any theory?

FREEDOM OF THOUGHT

It is telling that Acton is an author who is often cited only in bits and pieces, in aphorisms, rather than in a systematically coherent form. Notable quotes, as one finds in Wikipedia, are for many the only thing that has been passed down from the excessively educated Victorian age, when beards were long, libraries were paneled in dark wood and reached to the ceilings, and the people were so well-read as to intimidate us neo-barbarians. His most famous quotes include "Power tends to corrupt and absolute power corrupts absolutely"[5] and "liberty [is] not ... the power of doing what we like, but the right of being able to do what we ought."[6]

To reduce Acton to little sayings, an "Acton for Stressed-Out Managers," would do great injustice to him above all. Many Germans have long had a copy of Rudolf Eisler's *Kant-Lexikon* on their living room shelf.[7] Of course no one should ever be stopped from reading Kant in the original and as a whole, but should a person have forgotten what Kant means by the transcendental deduction of the concept of reason, an inquiring mind may just consult Eisler and find the relevant citations. Not to discount the meritorious work of brief

---

[5] Quoted from the Liberty Fund website (http://oll.libertyfund.org/pages/acton-creighton-correspondence-1887). Liberty Fund, Inc., a foundation of the libertarian philanthropist Pierre F. Goodrich, makes available (among other things) the works of Acton online and offers a discussion forum on its website of published texts. This quote, probably the most famous one of Acton, shows up in a posthumously published volume and is taken from a letter to Bishop Mandell Creighton dated 1887. It also can be found in *SW* 2:383.

[6] "The Roman Question," excerpted in *SW* 3:613.

[7] Rudolph Eisler, Kant-Lexikon, *Nachschlagewerk zu Kants sämtlichen Schriften, Briefen und handschriftlichen Nachlass* (Hildesheim: Olms, 1964).

anthologies like the one compiled by Alexander Dörrbecker,[8] but this does not work with Acton!

When it comes to the unique style of an author, the way he leads his reader into his thought, we can outline two basic types: the first type is characteristic of Aristotle and Kant, and the other is characteristic of Plato and Nietzsche. The first type speaks about or treats a certain subject, but the writings of other type are to be understood as an event instead. The fascinating thing about Plato is not his teaching about the ideas, but rather the way he uses dialogue between Socrates and his conversation partners to lead the reader to the truth, a technique known as maieutic (from the Greek word for midwifery). Plato's dialogues are events of truth. But these truths are only truths for a limited time. As soon as Plato puts an ironic comment into Socrates' mouth, the reader realizes that he has made the quest for truth too easy; the reader is pulled into a spiral movement, a vertical suction that leaves the reader "confused, but on a higher level."[9]

With Nietzsche it is the perspectivism that occurs in his texts. Naturally, he too makes comments about the necessary perspective of an insight or knowledge. For him, all insight or knowledge, not only the talk about it, is determined by the will to power. But the vital point is that Nietzsche pulls the rug out from under the reader; he tugs and pulls to get the reader to the other side and forces his reader to look at the world as he has known it from that perspective and to see the abyss in it. Nietzsche's dark *leitmotiv* that the reader learns about himself as he reads is, "How much blood and horror lies behind all 'good things.'"[10] One can study Kant and Aristotle, close the book, and gain significant insights, and yet everything is as it was before. After reading Plato and Nietzsche, the reader comes out as a changed person. How is it when reading Acton?

---

[8] *Geschichte und Freiheit. Ein Lord-Acton-Brevier*, ed. Alexander Dörrbecker (Zurich: Zurich Verlag, 2010).

[9] This quote is often attributed to Enrico Fermi, but there are also other possible sources. Cf. http://quoteinvestigator.com/2010/07/confused/.

[10] Friedrich Nietzsche, *The Genealogy of Morals*, in *The Birth of Tragedy and The Genealogy of Morals*, trans. Francis Golffing (Garden City, NY: Doubleday, 1956), 2.3 (p. 194).

Acton does not make it easy for his readers. The fact that no one has translated him into German yet cannot be attributed to him; rather, it is due to the German history of reception toward a British historian who did not see much value in the prevailing Prussian historiography of the nineteenth century. Acton devotes much time in his writings to the details of British history, which in the German science of history and its limited orientation are known only to specialists.[11] But the fact that Acton did not leave behind a larger body of work is entirely attributable to him. Many have speculated: Was it the overwhelming body of literature he had read and his unhealthy tendency to express great plans and force them through the eye of a needle?[12] Gertrude Himmelfarb speaks of the "grandiose nature of his ambitions."[13] Another explanation for his restless lack of productivity can be found in the fatal simultaneity of two goals that were nonsimultaneous: Acton wanted to be a person (of old) of great learning and knowledge of history in all fields at a time when the method of scientific precision was being established. This approach emphasized the small dimensions, the miniscule. To be precise: These two goals, one of breadth and the other of precision, met together in Acton himself and paralyzed each other. Acton sketched throughout his life projects of Herculean dimensions, starting with universal claims but lingering in the minutiae. These explanations are plausible, but they are still too extrinsic to Acton's work.

Acton is known as the historian of freedom. Freedom is the predominant theme, his life's theme. There are authors who write about freedom, and yet their texts (and the authors themselves) make it appear as though there were a barricade between themselves and their subject. John Stuart Mill wrote his magnum opus about liberty,

---

[11] The translation into German of some essential texts, as, for example, those in the edition by Gertrude Himmelfarb (*Essays on Freedom and Power* [Boston: Beacon, 1948]), is the foremost desideratum of a further study of Lord Acton.

[12] Mann, "Lord Acton," in *Zeiten und Figuren*, 38: "Acton's productivity suffered because of his excessive desire for knowledge—not only a desire to know everything about a subject, but also to know everything that was written about a subject, including what was not always worth reading."

[13] Himmelfarb, introduction to *Essays on Freedom and Power*, xxvii.

yet he remained throughout his life an employee of the East India Company—even after technically ceasing to be one. Acton, on the other hand, was different. He is in Nietzsche's emphatic sense a "free thinker," and freedom of thought is his genuine contribution to the liberal idea, which often brought forth enough thinkers who were not exactly in total control over their convictions. The freedom of Acton's thought shows itself primarily in his style and approach. His style is convoluted and full of digressions. Acton often jumps in with "pride, pomp and circumstance,"[14] as we read in Shakespeare's *Othello*, only to get lost in the labyrinth of history. He loves the academic side paths. But just as with the side paths in a park, you may end up somewhere you didn't intend to be, and you may see things from a new perspective. Acton never gets to the point, but exactly that is the point.

Acton is in no way the type of scholar who has such existential angst over his subject that he must use cross references, qualifiers, quotation marks, or the like, in order to get close to it. Acton does not fall on his knees before his subject. On the contrary, some of his theses are extremely pointed, even audacious. Himmelfarb states that his essays are "luxuriant in detail" but also "copious in superlatives."[15] And the way he wanders from one topic to another, which is very similar to the "digressive style" of another great English free thinker, Laurence Sterne, is not a lack of mental discipline. For one thing, it is the desire to indulge in testing one's thoughts against the reality of very different times and historic constellations. Acton is just as much an artist as a historian. His freedom of thought expresses itself in the most surprising comparisons as well as contradictions. Anyone who has had to experience firsthand the wasteland of uninspired history lectures or dull historical compendiums will feel revived when led by Acton into a free perspective on a given subject. Acton reminds us of Charles Dickens' first of the three spirits in *A Christmas Carol*, who drags the ornery Ebenezer Scrooge into his own beautiful as well as tragic past, to hold up this past in ever new, forgotten variations.

---

[14] William Shakespeare, *The Tragedy of Othello, the Moor of Venice*, act 3, scene 3.

[15] Himmelfarb, introduction to *Essays on Freedom and Power*, xxxiii.

Acton's freedom is that of an experimenter who does not stick to beaten paths but knows that the subject is not what directs the thoughts.

But this is not all just happy and arcadian. On the other hand, Acton's freedom of thought is rooted in being free of reassuring certainty in historical things, that is, in the *conditio humana* (human condition). The subjective freedom of his thought correlates with the objective of fate. For Acton nothing is static; everything can become its opposite at any time. This view is an expression of Acton's deep rooted skepticism. His basic instinct is that all human achievements are fragile. Acton's illustrations of the history of freedom or democracy make clear what close companions accomplishment and failure are; they also show how quickly a state of freedom can change into its opposite. Acton frequently uses the example of Athenian democracy turning into tyranny. During the classical times, under Pericles, the gods were the foundation of all law, but that changed when the sophists were in charge: "It was a very short step from the suspicion of Protagoras, that there were no gods, to the assertion of Critias that there is no sanction for laws. If nothing was certain in theology, there was no certainty in ethics and no moral obligation."[16] In the same text, Acton expresses his concern that a historiography that aims at following all subtle themes within the history of democracy will not contribute to peace and reconciliation: "Few discoveries are more irritating than those which expose the pedigree of ideas."[17] The idea of democracy was pushed forward by genius and error, by rule of law as well as crime; it is also "the truest friend of freedom" and "its most unrelenting foe."[18]

It is clear, then, why this kind of mercurial thinking is not often found in manuals and dictionaries of liberalism. His liberalism consists in declaring the certainties held by liberals (e.g., the continual progress in the constitution of liberty and the participation of the citizen) to be bad narratives. Acton knows too much. He sees too much. He

---

[16] Acton, "Sir Erskine May's *Democracy in Europe*," in *SW* 1:61.

[17] Acton, "Sir Erskine May's *Democracy in Europe*," in *SW* 1:55.

[18] Acton, "Sir Erskine May's *Democracy in Europe*," in *SW* 1:56: "Another conclusion ... is that democracy, like monarchy, is salutary within limits and fatal in excess; that it is the truest friend of freedom or its most unrelenting foe, according as it is mixed or pure."

is a historian and not a systematic philosopher, and his x-ray vision shines through prefabricated theory, even that of liberal theory.

FREEDOM OF CONSCIENCE

But we must not linger in hermeneutical considerations. In order to make a statement about Acton's contribution to the idea of liberalism, we must get to the very core of his statements. His meandering style however makes it somewhat difficult to locate the Archimedean point of his liberal thinking.

Each type of liberalism must ask itself why human beings should be free in the first place. Not only the Grand Inquisitor in Fyodor Dostoevsky's *The Brothers Karamazov* but also despots of all persuasions, such as warlords, ayatollahs, cardinals, party leaders, bosses, and family fathers—these are firmly convinced that freedom only unsettles people and that life would be better without it. Mill sets against this a simple and (to him) obvious explanation: humans are supposed be free, and politics and society are supposed to offer the general conditions for this because freedom increases the happiness of the individual and exists for the common benefit of society.

Acton's understanding of freedom is very different. Throughout his life he was an outcast in the club of liberals. This primarily was because he did not want to separate from his faith. In spite of all the church's open despotism and grotesque relationship to the truth, he did not leave the church, and he remained a deeply religious man until death. Since most mainstream liberals had lost their sense for the religious, they were unable to differentiate between the visible, institutional church and the invisible, spiritual church, the community of saints of all times. For them, church was and is an illiberal ruling organization.

To understand Acton better, I recommend rereading "The Grand Inquisitor," a piece that is interjected in Dostoevsky's *The Brothers Karamazov*.[19] In the interpretation of Christ's third temptation, especially, the Grand Inquisitor reflects on the nature of freedom that Christ gave to people. Yes, he makes John 8:32 ("you will know the truth,

---

[19] Fyodor Dostoevsky, *The Brothers Karamazov*, trans. Richard Pevear and Larissa Volokhonsky (London: Quartet Books, 1990), 246–64.

and the truth will make you free") the very center of Jesus' teaching. We can guess what the Grand Inquisitor thinks of this; it means that he rejects as naïve this ability to distinguish between good and evil and to allow good into one's heart. "With us," in other words, under the ruling of the church, "everyone will be happy.... Oh, we shall convince them that they will only become free when they resign their freedom to us, and submit to us."[20]

The freedom that Jesus spoke about and on which Acton bases his thoughts is the freedom of conscience. The conscience is the heart of his thinking about freedom. Acton's understanding of the conscience is thoroughly rooted in tradition. The Copernican revolution in how the concept of conscience was treated since Arthur Schopenhauer and then, in particular, by Ludwig Feuerbach and Nietzsche in the nineteenth century, never reached Acton. Acton descends into the treasure chambers of history and finds the origin of the concept of the conscience among the Stoics: "The true guide of our conduct is no outward authority, but the voice of God, who comes down to dwell in our souls.... True freedom, says the most eloquent of the Stoics, consists in obeying God."[21] This is still the church's teaching today: "conscience is man's most secret core and his sanctuary. There he is alone with God whose voice echoes in his depths."[22] From this vantage point, everything makes sense and finds its logical conclusion. From a hasty or secular perspective (which are really the same), the seemingly paradoxical statement that liberty is not the power of doing what we like, but the right of being able to do what we ought,[23] becomes completely understandable. In one of Acton's writings on freedom, he expresses this thought in more depth: "By liberty I mean the assurance that every man shall be protected in

---

[20] Dostoevsky, *Brothers Karamazov*, 258.

[21] Acton, "The History of Freedom in Antiquity," in *SW* 1:24.

[22] Second Vatican Council, Pastoral Constitution on the Church in the Modern World, *Gaudium et Spes* (December 7, 1965), 16; quoted in *Catechism of the Catholic Church*, § 1776, http://www.vatican.va/archive/ENG0015/_INDEX. HTM.

[23] See Acton, "The Roman Question," excerpted in *SW* 3:613.

doing what he believes his duty against the influence of authority and majorities, custom and opinion."[24]

This means that freedom always has two sides: the one side is that which results from the hermitage of one's conscience in dialogue with God, in other words, what the individual sees as a duty to be done before God. Acton, as a believer, looks at this moment of decision only in regard to other people, institutions, the state, and society as autonomous, but not in and of itself as autonomous. Because for Acton, when it comes to decisions of conscience, the individual looks to God as the sole authority. The other side has to do with the outward conditions in which the divine dialogue can take place.

CONDITIONS FOR FREEDOM

This is where Acton's contribution to the liberal school of thought actually begins. Liberalism, as we know it, is primarily concerned with protecting the individual, but what goes on inside the center core of the individual is of no concern. Here, in the discussion of resistance to inadmissible interference and encroachment, Acton once again appeals to a famous verse in the Bible: "Render to Caesar the things that are Caesar's, and to God the things that are God's" (Mark 12:17). Acton deduces from this verse a kind of doctrine of the spheres of freedom. According to this doctrine, freedom is always in danger when one of the two spheres, the political or the religious, is encroaching on the other. Accordingly, freedom is endangered when behavioral patterns of one sphere spread to the other, that is, when the political sphere is religiously loaded, or when the religious sphere is politicized.

Why does a loss of freedom result from this? We are used to thinking of the protection of rights as an intrinsic function of the political realm, in which the church and religious arena play no role. Yes, for many liberals, the church only intensifies the problem of lack of freedom—the church is, as is said today, part of the problem and not, as Acton says, part of the solution. In order to gain greater understanding of this, let's examine each part of the following definition by itself: "By liberty I mean the assurance that every man shall be

---

[24] Acton, "The History of Freedom in Antiquity," in *SW* 1:7.

protected in doing what he believes his duty against the influence of authority and majorities, custom and opinion."[25]

When it comes to the things that endanger freedom, Acton looks beyond the right to vote, representation, or federalism. Especially the last two terms are of great significance here: *custom* and *opinion*. It is easy for people today to imagine the lack of freedom in a world where the religious sphere is the only ruling one. We all know the horror scenarios depicted by Enlightenment figures, historical figures of the eighteenth century, and those today: a world of power hungry cardinals, moralizing family fathers, and pietistic grandmothers; a priest bows and scrapes at every negotiating table. For the British Catholic Acton, this is a world with a lack of freedom. He is far away from the conservative ultramontanism, which dreams of a world such as the one described above, only a little friendlier. This world lacks freedom because there is no escape from a definite, ideologically determined authority, because a clerically defined majority regulates what is known as custom and opinion. Acton is religious not in the sense of hoping for a world where everything bears the stamp of religion, but rather in that he would like to grant to the individual a realm, protected from everyone else, in which he can have a dialogue with God. The fact that he sees God's voice drowned out in such a theocratic world is the Enlightenment aspect—the British aspect, if you will—in Acton.

On the other hand, to put it simplistically, Acton's Catholicism, as well as his skepticism toward secularism and politics, needs to be explained too. It is much harder for people today to understand that the political sphere's reach can be threatening to freedom and that the religious sphere offers a needed place of refuge. We do not need to take time with the sufficiently familiar invectives against ancient tyranny, feudalism, and absolutism—everyone today can clearly see that. Have we not reached the highest form of freedom today in our system of free democracy? What can be a threat to our freedom, other than the "brown danger" of modern-day Nazis?

Acton does not primarily think of a free society as being endangered by the hands of its enemies, but rather through itself. In a "dialectic of Enlightenment" that is reminiscent of Theodor Adorno

---

[25] Acton, "The History of Freedom in Antiquity," in *SW* 1:7.

and Max Horkheimer, he takes up this subject at various places. This is expressed very concisely in Acton's writing "Sir Erskine May's *Democracy in Europe*." Contrary to what the title suggests, Acton does not really discuss May's book; rather, he uses the review as an excuse to develop his own thoughts (which is less objectionable than what many reviewers do).

A liberal who points out the dangers of democracy, can that still be a true liberal? Might he not be a fundamentalist conservative disguised as a liberal? Acton lived during a time when it was still possible to criticize democracy; when the horrors of the twentieth century had not yet taken place, which laughed in the face of democracy; and he lived in a country in which pluralism of thought had been alive and well, at least in the scientific world, if not always in the banking towers of Canary Wharf. The opening passages of Acton's review must seem rather strange to our political monoculture raised in democracy: "democracy, like monarchy, is salutary within limits and fatal in excess.... The effective distinction between liberty and democracy ... cannot be too strongly drawn.... [A] strange affinity has subsisted between democracy and religious persecution."[26]

In the following quote it becomes clearer what Acton means and what constitutes the danger to freedom in democracy. The pure view of institutions does not always provide any more help, as he comments in his other classic essay on freedom: "The history of institutions is often a history of deception and illusions; for their virtue depends on the ideas that produce and on the spirit that preserves them, and the form may remain unaltered when the substance has passed away."[27] The history of democracy is a process in which the political currency of "approval" gains more and more importance. Antagonistic feudal societies only need approval within the feudal bond; outside of it, nothing but pure violence reigns. Within democracy there is no inside or outside of the national state; approval becomes the only valid foundation for democracy's legitimacy. "A government entirely dependent on opinion looks for some security what that opinion shall be, strives

---

[26] Acton, "Sir Erskine May's *Democracy in Europe*," in *SW* 1:56.

[27] Acton, "The History of Freedom in Antiquity," in *SW* 1:6.

for the control of the forces that shape it, and is fearful of suffering the people to be educated in sentiments hostile to its institutions."[28]

The democratic state refrains from using oppression, force, and terror to reach the individual sphere of a person's conscience, but because the system must be supported by consensus, it will extend its reach to customs and opinions. The ruling majority of this democracy will do anything to preserve itself. It will try in every conceivable way to create the will of the majority. It must produce a climate in which dissenting opinions appear as a real threat to the system. "The true democratic principle, that every man's free will shall be as unfettered as possible, is taken to mean that free will of collective people shall be fettered in nothing."[29] Democracy has an inherent Jacobean, populist characteristic: it disregards convention, fails to think about the future, is jealous when it comes to talents and knowledge, and mistakes opinion for justice. "The old sovereigns of the world are exchanged for a new one, who may be flattered and deceived, but whom it is impossible to corrupt or to resist, and to whom must be rendered the things that are Caesar's and also the things that are God's."[30] The religious sphere—for Acton this is the power that guarantees freedom and conscience—comes under pressure from two sides: first, through a state that absorbs the church's sacredness into itself—political taboos and civil religion—and second, when the churches secularize themselves, joining in a dance around the political calf and making organizational matters the center.

But there is another level of reflection in Acton's thoughts, one in which he argues in the concrete terms of political science. If we include this view in our summary excursion and list which institutions Acton believes to be threats to freedom (e.g., the erosion of checks and balances through the moralizing of politics, the overemphasizing of equality and equalization of living conditions, the centralization and removal of federal structures, which function for Acton like firewalls against political encroachment of the state) then it becomes apparent that Acton's thoughts on threats to freedom under the conditions of absolute and social democracy are alarmingly relevant today.

---

[28] Acton, "Sir Erskine May's *Democracy in Europe*," in *SW* 1:57.

[29] Acton, "Sir Erskine May's *Democracy in Europe*," in *SW* 1:80.

[30] Acton, "Sir Erskine May's *Democracy in Europe*," in *SW* 1:80.

At this point, we should probably start a new section, a discussion about what status freedom has today. Such a discussion would have to explore the "paradox of freedom," namely, the fact that on the one hand, everything that liberals of the past have fought for appears to have been achieved. Not only in the political realm, but also in the personal realm, there never before has been more freedom of choice in the areas of products we consume, travel destinations, and personal orientation in all areas. On the other hand, almost casually, a shift in values has taken place. Is it possible that, at least in Germany, intellectual and political freedom is limited to an increasingly narrowing corridor of accepted views, outside of which one cannot count on any tolerance? Is it possible that the ever increasing contempt for the federal system—or, better said, for regional stakeholders and their alleged shortcomings (as opposed to the great desire to be released from central control by the state) under the seal of approval for increased efficiency and optimization—is a restriction of freedom?

What hides behind the notion that classical thoughts about freedom in light of the economic realities and security challenges of our times was nothing but a fair weather philosophy? These are tempting but frivolous questions, since the perspective from which one would have to answer them cannot be taken yet. But what does it mean that the liberal now looks like a caricature at best and that government regulation and security make him appear anachronistic, even as a threat to freedom? Is this a movement against the exaggerations of the use of freedom in certain areas of commerce?

Or might it be an anticipated emergency legislation, to secure freedom by restricting freedom? Do the exchange rate losses of liberalism (it really is too soon to speak of the end of liberalism) mean that freedom itself has fallen into disrepute? Doesn't anyone see that behind the flickering appearance of the "little" freedom of choice there is a homogenization and uniformity, which Nietzsche recognized in the "the last man" and Peter Sloterdijk in the "human park"?

To end an article about Acton, this great enthusiast of freedom and explorer of history, on such a grim note does not do justice to its subject. Acton the historian was always opposed to the affectation of interpreting one's own time. The history of "the paradox of freedom" still needs to be written.

3

RELIGIOUS FOUNDATIONS
OF THE LIBERAL SOCIETY

Freedom and Conscience*

Christoph Böhr

Translated by Victoria Huizinga

L ord Acton was not a philosopher and never saw himself as one. He was a historian of ideas and therefore submerged himself deeply in philosophical issues. The history of freedom was at the very center of his scholarly work, and the quest to define and understand freedom was the cord that tied his various professional occupations as publicist, parliamentarian, and professor together.

Students of the history of freedom must put at the center of their study an idea that, in the attempt to identify this term, gave philosophy some of its most significant accomplishments. Hardly any other term has inspired European philosophy to a greater degree, for a longer time, and with more controversy than the question of what constitutes humanity's yearning for freedom. Therefore, students of the history of freedom have no choice but to wrestle deeply with this central philosophical term. This is precisely what Lord Acton

---

*A longer version of this essay was originally published in German as "Die religiösen Grundlagen der liberalen Gesellschaft. Lord Acton über Freiheit und ihre Gründung in der Wahrheit des Gewissens—eine Vergegenwärtigung," in *Glaube, Gewissen, Freiheit. Lord Acton und die religiösen Grundlagen der liberalen Gesellschaft*, ed. Christoph Böhr, Philipp W. Hildmann, and Johann Christian Koecke (Wiesbaden: Springer, 2015), 261–91.

did. His account of freedom is at the same time a wrestling with the term itself and a perusal of freedom's historical development. Acton reflects on the very foundations of freedom, as is evident especially (but not exclusively) in his two most important works on freedom.[1] The following discussion explores the question of how Acton as a liberal thinker follows the idea,[2] as well as how he understands and explains it: What is freedom—and what do we mean when this term enters our thought and our speech?

Acton wrestled with answering exactly this question his whole life. His answer is that freedom is the assurance that everyone is protected to do what they believe they ought to do, even if it means having to act against authorities, majorities, customs, habits, and opinions.[3] As used here, the term *assurance* does not refer to a subjective feeling; rather, it focuses on objective circumstances. Unequivocally critical of the state, Acton adds that the purpose of the state is to protect liberty—against governments and majorities.[4] The state is empowered to determine duties, and to draw the line between good and evil, but

---

[1] "The History of Freedom in Antiquity," in *SW* 1:5–28; and "The History of Freedom in Christianity," in *SW* 1:29–53.

[2] Benjamin Disraeli was a Tory and, as such, a political opponent to Acton. He identified as a Whig and rather accurately identified a difference between following an idea or a principle. Cf. the comment in Disraeli's speech in the House of Commons on June 5, 1848 (which admittedly was not aimed at Acton personally but, considering the differences in their thought, aimed at the position Acton held): "My objection to Liberalism is this—that it is the introduction into the practical business of life of the highest kind—namely, politics—of philosophical ideas instead of political principles" (*House of Commons Debate*, June 5, 1848, in *House of Commons Debates*, vol. 99 [1848], 385ff. [quote on p. 396]).

Regarding the reason for giving precedence to idea over principle, cf. Acton, Add. Mss. 4945, p. 280, excerpted in *SW* 3:499: "Very late in human history, Liberty appears, defended for itself all along the line. That can only be when ideas prevail, and not interests or traditions." Principles are never timeless the way ideas are; they are always tied to tradition and conditioned by history.

[3] Acton, "The History of Freedom in Antiquity," in *SW* 1:7; cf. Acton's definition of liberty in *SW* 3:489–91.

[4] Acton to Richard Simpson, October 8, 1861, in *CLARS* 2:182.

only in its own immediate jurisdictions. Outside of these (narrowly set) boundaries, the state has only the right to help people in their struggle for survival in an indirect way, by promoting and supporting the influence of the kinds of institutions that, in the face of temptation to do evil, will prevail so that every temptation to do evil can be resisted—specifically, the institutions of religion and education and the distribution of wealth.

Two things are notable regarding this definition: Liberty is for Acton first of all an essential precondition for religion. The state is not religion and the state should not make the objectives of religion its own. Instead the relationship between state and religion is marked by the state's interest to foster and protect the independence of religion, because this will help people to resist temptation: "liberty, by this definition, is the essential condition and guardian of religion."[5] To continue this thought, we see that religion is the counterpart of the state,[6] neither an extension of it nor a reason for its self-justification. Religion helps people in the struggle of life—alongside education and the distribution of wealth. The fact that Acton in this context mentions education should not surprise us. But what is remarkable is the third pillar of his argument, which Acton sees as supporting the defense against seduction and temptation: the distribution of wealth. Acton, especially as a liberal, was not a proponent of a sprawling welfare state. But he recognized that the state, whose power he thought should really be kept at a minimum, can best exercise this restrained authority[7] when the society does not sink into poverty and misery. In order to ensure liberty, living conditions need to be adequate. Without delving deeper into this thought, which may appear more obvious today than in Acton's day,[8] it should be mentioned here that Acton's

---

[5] Acton, "The History of Freedom in Antiquity," in *SW* 1:7.

[6] Acton, Add. Mss. 4869, p. 20, excerpted in *SW* 3:611: "It is the union of Church and State that has caused all persecution."

[7] Cf. Acton, "The History of Freedom in Antiquity," in *SW* 1:14: "for liberty, justice, and equal laws, it is ... necessary that Democracy should restrain itself."

[8] Cf. Acton, "Sir Erskine May's *Democracy in Europe*," in *SW* 1:54ff. Otherwise the danger threatens that is known from history: "religion flourished, but failed to reach [the masses of the people]" (*SW* 1:81).

definition of the term is not without further consequences: freedom also means not being subjected to the regulations imposed by the state,[9] which means that religion, which requires freedom from the state, in turn becomes the guarantee of this freedom, because, as the counterpart to the state, it also creates the distance that is necessary to limit the claims of the state.

Acton describes liberty as a politically conditioned concept, not as an unconditioned philosophical one: "Liberty is essentially a conditioned term that cannot be independent from the law."[10] But the rationale of freedom, even though we can only describe it according to historically contingent conditions, reaches into the unconditional. It has its roots in an experience that does not appear to be conditioned by history but is an expression of unconditionality in its purest form: it is the experience of the certainty of the conscience. Freedom flourishes in connection to the conscience.[11] Acton does not tire of continually stressing this thought. "Liberty of conscience is the first of liberties," he writes, and he gives the reason for this statement: "because it is the liberty to avoid sin."[12] A person is free when without outward obstructions he is able to evade the temptations of evil within himself and resist the the seduction of sin. In order to do this, he must be free and must not be forced in one direction or another.

[9] Cf. Acton, Add. Mss. 5611, n. n., excerpted in *SW* 3:492: "Liberty is the supreme law. Limited only by greater liberty."

[10] Ulrich Noack, *Politik als Sicherung der Freiheit: Nach den Schriften von John Dalberg-Acton, dem Historiker der Freiheit, 1834–1902* (Frankfurt am Main: Schulte-Bulmke, 1947), 209.

[11] Acton, Add. Mss. 4916, p. 11, excerpted in *SW* 3:557: "So we may say that [liberty] flourishes jointly with conscience. Decay of the one brings about decay of the other."

[12] Acton, Add. Mss. 4870, p. 9, excerpted in *SW* 3:504; cf. also Add. Mss. 4901, p. 242, excerpted in *SW* 3:504: "Conscience [is] the means of emancipation from the servitude of sin." The expression "the first of liberties" is very similar to the identification of freedom of conscience as "freedom of all freedoms" made by Benedict XVI. In his message on the World Day of Peace in 2011 he summarized religious freedom as the "synthesis and keystone" of all basic rights and freedoms; that is why (and he recalled a statement from his predecessor, John Paul II) it is "the litmus test for the respect of all other human rights."

In order not to succumb to the inward bondage of sin, it is necessary not to be seduced to it by an outward bondage.

Acton points to the indissoluble connection between interior and exterior freedom. Freedom of conscience also constitutes freedom of action. The interior direction must not be dictated by political authorities: "The true guide of our conduct is no outward authority, but the voice of God, who comes down to dwell in our souls, who knows all our thoughts, to whom are owing all the truth we know, and all the good we do; for vice is voluntary, and virtue comes from the grace of the heavenly spirit within."[13] Before we dismiss such sentences as the stuff of faith (which they undoubtedly do contain), one should bear in mind the logic of this thought: What, asks Acton, justifies the freedom of people to remain undisturbed by the state and other authorities in regard to what they do at their own discretion? Why is the negative freedom of independence from paternalism the prerequisite for all the subsequent positive freedom for self-determination? Acton's answer is this: because human beings in their decision to act follow a claim that is more unconditional than any servitude that the state and politics expect from citizens. "True freedom, says the most eloquent of the Stoics, consists in obeying God."[14]

Therefore, awareness of the conscience brings freedom from external coercion and thus demands religious freedom and the guarantee of social freedom. Our conscience demands that our conscience and also that of other people be respected. "Therefore it tends to restrict authority and to enlarge liberty. It is the law of self-government."[15] The voice of God speaks in the conscience; to be precise, the conscience is each person's subjective perception of an objective claim to validity. Human beings can err in their perception of this claim. But that does not change the fact that only the voice of conscience gives a certainty that is lasting and binding and cannot be circumvented. In this sense it is God's announcement to human beings—their only

---

[13] Acton, "The History of Freedom in Antiquity," in *SW* 1:24.

[14] Acton, "The History of Freedom in Antiquity," in *SW* 1:24.

[15] Acton, Add. Mss. 4901, p. 254, excerpted in *SW* 3:504; cf. also Add. Mss. 5604, p. 30, excerpted in *SW* 3:490: "Liberty: Power over oneself. Opposite: Power over others."

access to the *mundus intelligibilis*[16]—and the self-attestation of human beings in the face of all attempts to be objectified, utilized, and used. The commandment of the conscience supersedes every commandment of the state because the conscience is regarded as unconditional. Thus the conscience does not point out limitations to freedom; rather, it puts them to work. Consequently the decay of the conscience leads to the collapse of freedom.

The prerequisite for freedom is found in the conscience, the ability to differentiate, and the attention paid to options from which one can choose. "I can, but I don't have to": this inner voice of the person already played a great role in antiquity (Acton frequently points to Stoicism) and later became the crucial point in the understanding of the term *good* in Christianity. A person may not stand in the way of or even block what the conscience demands. Freedom is the right, and the requirement,[17] to follow the conscience at any time—that is, to do what we ought to do.

One consequence of this way of defining the relationship between conscience and freedom is that no interests of any kind may limit a person's rights. Nothing and no one has the authority to interfere with the voice of the conscience. Exactly because Acton (like John Henry Newman) awards the highest rank to the conscience, it is important to understand that the conscience is not what people today often think it means—an ultimate justification informed by the inclinations of the moment. Those who invoke their conscience today often want to be left in peace and be spared further inquiries. But the reference to conscience means something entirely different, namely, a reference to an order or system that follows truth and not the whim of the day.

---

[16] Cf. Christoph Böhr, "Die Selbsterfahrung des Handelns in der Unvereinbarkeit des Lebens. Zur Wiederentdeckung von Kants 'novus rerum ordo' der Philosophie," in *Facetten der Kantforschung. Ein Internationaler Querschnitt*, Festschrift für Nobert Hinske zum 80. Geburtstag, ed. Christoph Böhr and Heinrich P. Delfosse (Stuttgart-Bad Cannstatt: Frommann-Holzboog, 2011), 11ff.

[17] Acton, Add. Mss. 4939, p. 326, excerpted in *SW* 3:491: "Liberty is the condition which makes it easy for Conscience to govern. Liberty is government of Conscience. Reign of conscience." Next to this condition of freedom, that the conscience be followed, an additional condition is needed, namely, the will to heed the conscience.

Today the term *conscience* is an expression of subjectivity—and it is that as well, the uncircumventable self-attestation of a human being and one's ultimate convictions.[18] But conscientious reasons can only enforce such a self-attestation when it expresses a proven conviction that is measured by truth. This is what is meant when we speak of the voice of the conscience being the divine speech inside human beings. The conscience is the advocate of truth—the sole truth, not the expression of a whim, an opinion, or a state of mind. And it is strictly because of this that the conscience demands the external freedom to be able to do what it insists upon doing or, even more often, not doing. This is where Acton sees the measure of freedom, which corresponds with the measure of conscience both in religious as well as political questions. What the inner voice of the conscience demands is to be guaranteed externally by freedom. The inner authority of the human conscience gives limits to the external authority of power. The conscience makes the truth known; both determine the extent and magnitude of freedom, and in that sense, both together bring forth freedom.

Acton stands in the tradition of natural law, as it was developed in the first centuries after Christ up to Thomas Aquinas,[19] a tradition that ascribed to freedom the highest position in the structural framework of human communal life. In the conscience we recognize what is right. What conscience is to recognition, freedom is to the system of communal life: it is the criterion of its authenticity and the origin of its truth. The right to freedom in its external, finite possibilities is grounded in the absolute, the voice of truth in the conscience.

---

[18] Cf. Christoph Böhr, "Freiheit zu aller Freiheit. Zum Grund der Gründung unseres zeitgenössischen Verfassungs Denken," *Logos i Ethos* 18, no. 2 (2014): 153ff.

[19] Acton, "The History of Freedom in Christianity," in *SW* 1:34, quotes Thomas Aquinas: "There is no security for us as long as we depend on the will of another man." And Acton continues: "This language ... contains the earliest exposition of the Whig theory." F. A. Hayek refers to this evaluation, which is hardly shared by many contemporary liberals: "In some respects Lord Acton was not being altogether paradoxical when he described Thomas Aquinas as the first Whig" (*The Constitution of Liberty* [Chicago: The University of Chicago Press, 1960], 457n4).

Acton sees in the conscience the starting point from which every search for human order proceeds: it gives reason for freedom, cries for freedom, and fills with freedom. It is in the clarification of the concept of the conscience, which cannot be constrained by limits precisely because of the certainty that the conscience conveys, where we see that Acton's scientific and historical points of view flow together with his convictions about Christian doctrine. For him the study of the humanities is the best weapon in the fight for the truth of faith. In 1863, in the context of summarizing a paper that Ignaz von Döllinger delivered at the Munich congress for theologians, Acton calls Origen, who was born in Alexandria and presumably died in Tyros as a result of torture, the father of "Christian science."[20] His influence on—and in—the history of theology and philosophy cannot be overestimated.[21] This has not just formal but, even more so, material grounds. Origen was not only the first Christian theologian, but more importantly, he was the true originator and founder of a Christian philosophy, by reason of the subject matter. "These contents hang together with his teaching on freedom. Freedom—that is the central theme, out of which proceed all other philosophical contents. Therefore, Origen is

---

[20] Cf. Johann Joseph Ignaz von Döllinger, *Verhandlungen der Versammlung katholischer Gelehrten in München vom 28. September bis 1. Oktober 1863* (Regensburg: G. J. Manz, 1863), 26–27. Döllinger makes reference here to the "scientific paternity" that Origen accords to all theology even though his "deep and wide reaching" errors in doctrinal matters consisted in the fact that he forgot what theology always has to be aware of: that it carries "its treasure in earthen vessels" and therefore requires "the continual observation and correction that comes from the general doctrinal consciousness of the Church" in order "to prevent arrogance, which every human science tends to be tempted by." Acton summarizes this statement in "The Munich Congress," in *SW* 3:215: "The grave dogmatic errors of Origen, the father of Christian science ..., served as a warning ... that the intellectual study of religious truth needs the watchful supervision of the Church."

[21] For a good overview, see Ulrich Berner, *Origenes* (Darmstadt: Wissenschaftliche Buchgesellschaft, 1981).

the philosopher of freedom within the philosophy of antiquity, and that applies in comparison to pagan philosophy."[22]

Origen thought of truth as a freedom that is generally accessible and incarnate in humans. This incarnation was fulfilled completely in the union of the historical Christ with the absolute Logos. Because this Logos indwells all people and is irrevocably appropriated in them, human beings are led to a certain autonomy before God. Origen was a Neoplatonist, and in light of his Neoplatonic philosophy, which was followed by a considerable part of the Catholic theology of the day, the nature of humans is determined by their share in the Logos. As a result, this relationship of participation,[23] which lies in the nature of all human beings, applies universally. Specifically, it is universal, without exception, and indestructible. This nature, however, is the freedom to which every person is called. "God wants the realization of what is good only under the condition of freedom. The good that God wants is at odds with natural necessity and the laws of causality. That is why the good that God wants is actually nothing other than freedom itself.... God does not put in place set natures by means of a dark decree of providence, one to his honor the other to his dishonor, but he wants nothing else but freedom, which can certainly miss its target."[24]

---

[22] Theo Kobusch, "Origenes, der Initiator der Christlichen Philosophie," in *Origenes, vir ecclesiasticus*, ed. Wilhelm Geerlings and Hildegard König (Bonn: Borengässer, 1995), 35.

[23] Regarding the meaning of the concept expressed by the German word *Teilhabe* (participation) and its analogous use by Origen, cf. Gerhard Gruber, *Zoē: Wesen, Stufen und Mitteilung des wahren Lebens bei Origenes* (Munich: Max Hueber, 1962), 212: "This participation [*Teilhabe*] justifies applying the name of a good both to the one who completely possesses it as well as to all those who possess it to a lesser degree.... Using another pair of concepts, the contrast between full and shared ownership can be expressed as substantial and accidental ownership." This means that he receives a genuine share in the substance of the one who meets the recipient in the role of giver (Gruber, *Zoē*, 217). In precisely this sense, Acton sees humans as having a genuine share in the substance of God with and in their conscience.

[24] Kobusch, "Origenes, der Initiator der Christlichen Philosophie," 41.

This statement could have been made by Acton, whose occupation with Origen—probably sparked by his teacher Döllinger—likely reached far deeper than has been documented so far. When human nature is recognized and defined—apart from all necessities—as freedom, one cannot get around a voluntaristic view of evil: the origin of evil lies within human beings, in their will.[25] The inner self makes a decision[26] and finds its freedom. Gregory of Nyssa later adopted this view of freedom and said that humans, as beings that abuse their freedom, are the creators and originators of evil, and "that means that as such they still possess their own dignity."[27]

The implication of this definition of human beings in their "nature of freedom" is obvious and was described by Origen: he substantiates the conscience as ontological and identifies it with regards to the share that each human being has in the Logos by nature and, thus, in and with his freedom. To be more exact, Origen identifies the conscience with the pneuma of the Logos, with a power that is at work in humans and exercises influence over a person's conscience, soul, and action. This power is the source of all recognition of what ought to be. In other words, it is the place of true distinction between good and evil. It is that ability that was called synderesis[28] by high

----

[25] This is of course also true for the decision to do good in the sense of an affirmation of the soul of human beings, which was originally created good; cf. Origen, *Against Celsus*, in *Ante-Nicene Fathers*, ed. Alexander Roberts and James Donaldson, vol. 4 (New York: Scribner's, 1907), 3.69 (p. 491).

[26] The differentiation of the inner and the exterior self is the precondition for developing the concept of conscience. Therefore for Origen it plays a great role. Cf. Ulrich Volp, *Die Würde des Menschen: Ein Beitrag zur Anthropologie in der Alten Kirche* (Leiden: Brill, 2006), esp. 143ff.

[27] Kobusch, "Origenes, der Initiator der christlichen Philosophie," 42; cf. 43. On the "metaphysics of the inner self" in Origen and those following him, cf. also Theo Kobusch, *Christliche Philosophie: Die Entdeckung der Subjektivität* (Darmstadt: Wissenschaftliche Buchgesellschaft, 2006), esp. 142ff.

[28] Cf. Ludger Honnefelder, "Vernunft und Gewissen. Gibt es eine philosophische Begründung für die Normativität des Gewissens?," in *Der Streit um das Gewissen*, ed. Gerhard Höver and Ludger Honnefelder (Paderborn: F. Schöningh, 1993), 113ff. (here quoting p. 120), concerning the relationship to truth reflected by the conscience:

medieval philosophy and is often and by no means incorrectly translated as "conscience."

The thought of this incarnation of the freedom of the eternal Word in the nature of the finite human being is so groundbreaking because it establishes the universality of the human ability to make distinctions. The origin of decisions based on conscience is not one's intellectual powers or spiritual talent but rather one's freedom—the nature of human beings, which without exception is the nature of each person.[29] Every person, regardless of transgressions and aberrations, remains in this nature, which he cannot destroy or lose. Even in their deepest guilt, people still have a share in the divine logos, which has become irrevocably incarnate in them and in their freedom. Humans are unable to dispose of this participation;[30]

Only insight into the first principles, as habitually supplied by practical reason (Thomas is speaking here of 'original knowledge,' synderesis), is infallibly true. The ethical judgment reflected in the conscience's judgment, in contrast, by virtue of how it operates is not just subject to the possibility of rationalizing in error or making assumptions for incorrect or unconvincing reasons; it also can come to differing conclusions without errors of form or content as it considers reasons and rules—all the more as the rules to be considered become increasingly concrete.

[29] Cf. Origen, *Against Celsus*, 3.69 (p. 491): "We ... know of only one nature in every rational soul, and ... maintain that none has been created evil by the Author of all things, but that many have *become* wicked through education, and perverse example, and surrounding influences, so that wickedness has been naturalized in some individuals."

[30] Ulrich Noack, *Katholizität und Geistesfreiheit, nach den Schriften von John Dalberg-Acton, 1834–1902* (Frankfurt am Main: G. Schulte-Bulmke, 1936), 182, notes that this Catholic doctrine, "according to which the gift of grace [i.e., innate freedom] belongs to human nature, which was *never completely destroyed*," also influenced the doctrine of original sin at the Council of Trent: "As part of the freedom of the will, the free participation in the sanctification of the earthly life also remained intact. One can see here the deep Catholic foundation for Acton's thoughts on freedom, also as they pertain to the political realm" (emphasis in original).

they must make use of their freedom.[31] The natural order—in other words, human freedom—is to be considered universal, and this can be understood as the presupposition for all debates on natural law, which simultaneously draws an insurmountable border against all gnostic and Marcionite tendencies.

In this anthropology, which Acton links with Origen for good reason,[32] is a fine-edged foundation for the evidence for what we today call the sanctity of human dignity, and this foundation is already found in the first three centuries after Christ, even in several syntheses of Stoicism and Neoplatonism. Acton, who probably knew this terminology from Döllinger,[33] considered this to be in essence the

---

[31] We cannot delve here into what all lies behind this statement. It is directed, in a specific and narrow sense, at the self-creation of humans; not in the way contemporary constructivism conceives of this self-creation, but strictly in the understanding held by both Pico della Mirandola (as well as Eberhard Schockenhoff, *Zum Fest der Freiheit: Theologie des christlichen Handelns bei Origenes* [Mainz: Matthias-Grünewald-Verlag, 1990], 309) and Immanuel Kant (e.g., the third proposition in his "Idea for a Universal History with a Cosmopolitain Aim" [1784]). Jerome Gaith, *La conception de la liberté chez Grégoire de Nysse* (Paris: J. Vrin, 1953), mentions that one can hear in Origen the Jean-Paul Sartre of Christian antiquity, as Kobusch cleverly states ("Origenes, der Initiator der Christlichen Philosophie," 43) in an allusion to Sartre's statement that human beings are "condemned" to freedom.

[32] Cf. Noack, *Katholizität und Geistesfreiheit*, 181–82:

> What is greatly effective is ... the central idea of Origen of innate freedom, of which reason is a part. This combination is seen in what it means to be created in the likeness of God, and makes up the autonomy of human beings in comparison to God. Because this 'wonderful nature' of human beings is also to be understood as a gift of grace, one of deepest sources for the Catholic-liberal view of freedom remained open, one of the inexhaustible powers that enthralled the young Acton in his reading of Origen and accompanied him to the final summit of his scientific refinement.

One can even go a step further and say that the historian of freedom, Acton, found his understanding of the term *freedom* by reading the philosopher of freedom, Origen.

[33] The concept "dignity" as well as "inviolability" can indeed already be found in Döllinger. Cf. Johann Joseph Ignaz von Döllinger, *Christenthum und Kirche in der Zeit der Grundlegung*, (Regensburg: G. J. Manz, 1868), 408–9:

foundation for the sanctity of conscience, which he in turn held to be synonymous with the sanctity of human freedom.

Acton diagnoses in Christian doctrine a definite impulse towards emphasizing human freedom—an impulse that remains in effect even when Christianity itself and its organization in the form of self-declared ecclesiasticism appears to be losing sight of this impulse. During such times, the liberal impulse, which Christianity embraced as its own, shows itself in a different way, namely, not individually-anthropologically, but institutionally-politically, in antithesis to ecclesiastical and secular power and vice versa. Even in the darkest times of church history[34] it remained undisputed that the synthesis of the divine and human—seen from a Christian perspective—is to be seen exactly where antiquity and the pagan world saw and suspected it the least: in the nature of human beings (more precisely, in the human's ontological status); and in fact not where antiquity and the pagan world up to that time had presumed it to be: in the constitution of the state, politics, and culture—in short, in the unity of throne and altar.

Christianity combines the divine and the human condition on the level of being and precisely not in the sense of a synthesis between politics and religion. It distinguishes between two systems of rule: the divine on the one hand and the secular on the other. And exactly this distinction has been the source of fierce controversy over many centuries. Origin and his followers were particularly shaped by this view,

> Those who looked closely enough, even in the apostolic age, could sense that the Christian church was destined to become the school and educational center for true civil freedom. The true concept of freedom and the sense of it had not been present in the pre-Christian world—specifically, freedom based on the recognition of a foreign equality and of the dignity and inviolability of the individual person.... True freedom was first introduced to the world via Christianity: the right of free self-determination with which human beings respect and recognize the same freedom for other people, moving away from the egoistic pursuit of using other people merely as unfree tools only to advance one's own pleasures and benefit and, in the entire area of human activity that is under the direction of the conscience, follow only their own insight and their own will, not the will of another.

[34] Cf. Acton, Add. Mss. 5006, p. 63, excerpted in *SW* 3:609: These were the times "when the right of conscience, the duty of obeying it, was not admitted."

and this experience was not without consequences for his thinking about God and the world. It was a painful controversy, a struggle for power and influence, the history of a rivalry that saw itself as a struggle for sub- and superordination. Acton recalled in countless writings the various facets of this history—and interpreted it as history on the way to freedom. He became a historiographer of the the ups and downs between religion and politics in their battle for predominance and supremacy. The distinction between the matters of this world and spiritual matters, so deeply rooted in Christian thought, occasionally fell into disrepair[35] but always prevailed in the end.

Acton's view of this argument does not correspond with the point of view that is common today, which struggles in this battle to find an inner direction. It was clear to Acton that out of this rivalry between these two claims to power and systems of rule the fountain of freedom bubbles up—religious as well as political freedom, the "occidental freedom" to which Acton was devoted more than anything else. And because this freedom, which finds its origin in the divine aspect of the conscience, is threatened by power especially, he could not help but do everything possible to stand against the dogma of infallibility created by Vatican I, which for him was the desperate and unsuccessful attempt to salvage a claim to power.

It is the nature of the above mentioned Christian understanding of the synthesis of the divine and secular in the nature of humans (i.e., ontological, on the level of being) that made the battle between emperor and pope possible in the first place. The dispute for supremacy and predominance exists precisely because religion and politics cannot be brought to a synthesis. Acton considered the history of this dispute between these two powers wielding the sword to be synonymous with the history of—and leading to—freedom. He is probably right, because the result of this dispute led to the mutual limitation of power that made space for freedom.

In his study "The History of Freedom in Christianity" Acton describes knowledgeably the course of this conflict. Rémi Brague refers approvingly to Acton's summary account of these centuries-

---

[35] Cf. the excellent and complete overview by Martin Rhonheimer, *Christentum und säkularer Staat: Geschichte—Gegenwart—Zukunft* (Freiburg im Breisgau: Herder, 2012).

long conflicts: it is possible that this controversy between the secular and spiritual realm enabled

> Europe to preserve its uniqueness, which is in fact an unprecedented historical phenomenon. The significance of this was recognized by John Emerich Edward Dalberg Lord Acton.... This conflict prevented Europe from changing into one of those empires that in constant self-reflection claimed to have borne and to embody an ideology according their own custom fit and imagination. The independence of the religious from the political realm made it possible for Europe to open itself like a ripe fruit and to pass its religious content on to other cultural territories even after the political ties had been broken off. In this way the secular realm and its system received a space in which it could develop according to its own laws. That's not to say that the secular system could develop without any regard to ethics.... Ethics provided the frame of the secular system; but just like every frame, it sets only negative limits and does not provide a positive set of rules.[36]

Brague both stands in Acton's wake with this statement and also continues Acton's thought. Indeed it seems that the polarity of religion and politics, which began to develop in Europe with the appearance of Christianity, created a unique culture worldwide that gave room to freedom. The tendency of politics to follow its own laws, according to Brague, was only fenced in by religion as if by a frame. Religion in Europe does not inform politics but fences it in. Into the place of the inspiration of antiquity there steps in the Christian domestication of politics by means of religion. To think this way is Christian—and liberal. Christianity and liberalism coincide in this point. And this explains how a former Whig—as was Acton[37]—can be a Christian through and through.

---

[36] Rémi Brague, *Europa—seine Kultur, seine Barbarei: Exzentrische Identität und römische Sekundarität*, ed. Christoph Böhr (Wiesbaden: VS Verlag für Sozialwissenschaften, 2012), 181–82.

[37] Acton, Add. Mss. 4946, p. 253, excerpted in *SW* 3:536: "Whigs: They were defenders of liberty who defended it for the sake of religion. The union

The distance of religion from the whole political realm makes not only human beings but also religion itself free and independent from political considerations and from power games. According to Brague, this is where the influence of the religion of the Europeans, namely, Christianity, lies. The less this religion has to carry politics on its shoulders, the easier it is for it to make a home in other cultures. One could pointedly say that what is fascinating about Europe proceeds from the freedom that was fought for by the religion of the Europeans and takes root in it. Its politics do not appear more stimulating and interesting; as a battle for the self-assertion of power[38] it is hardly any different from the politics of other cultures. But the anthropology of the Europeans, which is a result of their religion, persuades compellingly today more than ever before.

The intention here is not to promote a rose-colored way of looking at things. Anyone who glanced even briefly at the history of the European continent and the history of its religion knows about the many errors and tribulations on the way to freedom. Moreover this struggle for freedom did not stop some Europeans from engaging in the most murderous bloodshed of the twentieth century that has ever taken place in human history. To close our eyes to this would be foolish and blind. And yet this recognition should not deceive us and cause us to overlook the fact that the two ideologies that were most responsible, National Socialism and Communism, cost millions of people their lives because these ideologies betrayed, and nullified, precisely this indissoluble separation between politics and religion. Both ideologies were political religions, which gave politics a (pseudo-) religious orientation. In other words, they were sustained by a quasi-religious faith that became all the stronger the more the European religion that was recognized until then (i.e., Christianity) became persecuted, just as was in accord with both ideologies' strategy. Having said that, it must be pointed out that it has been only a

---

of the two things constituted the Whigs."

[38] This is what Acton means when he describes the politics of his time. Cf. Acton, Add. Mss. 5528, p. 170, excerpted in *SW* 3:564: Politics "is treated nowadays as a thing purely empirical, a matter not of theory but of practice only."

few decades since this attempt to betray Europe and its heritage of freedom that had been described by Acton.

What distinguishes this description of Europe's history in Acton's mind is the fact that it breaks with all the classifications, ideologizations, and typologizings of its time. Terms such as *liberalism, conservatism, socialism,* or *nationalism* are not what he uses to give meaning to his own thoughts or the thinking of others; rather, his starting point is the anthropocentric starting point that is in human beings themselves—their conscience, their self-determination, and, coming from these, the claim to a guarantee of their freedom. These are what give him the standard by which to judge the legitimacy of any system.

Acton does not embed himself in the trenches of a historico-philosophical ivory tower; rather, he liberates political theory from the ballast of excessive normativity by pointing it to the real subject matter: the path to the human being, whose position always deserves respect. Every system of communal life needs to follow that. This respect has a name: freedom. It is at the same time the result as well as the prerequisite of religion.

Accordingly, those who care about religion—especially the Christian religion—must profess a commitment to human beings and their freedom. Those who despise religion will not be able to follow this thought. But even they will not be able to escape Acton's historical analyses. What, except for the conscience, a person's inner self-attestation, would place external freedom on solid ground? What finally gives a person certainty is only the immediate experience of conscience as an absolute and unconditional answer to the question of what is right. Acton, one could say, worked out a liberalism that knows about its religious foundation and has resulted in a conviction today that has become the very center of secular and liberal democracy,[39] even if it does not always make itself obvious. No law is protected by contemporary constitutional order nearly as much as the freedom to appeal to one's conscience.

---

[39] Cf. Acton, Add. Mss. 4939, p. 39, excerpted in *SW* 3:553: "The essence of democracy: to esteem the rights of others as one's own.... It received a glorious sanction from Christianity." But because democracy tends toward despotism, "absolute democracy" is synonymous with the downfall of freedom.

It would be very worthwhile to explore in some depth the consideration, which Acton took over from Döllinger with conviction, that Origen was the father of a "Christian science." As far as I know, that has not yet been done, except for the insightful comments by Ulrich Noack along these lines. Maybe Noack's insights are so compelling in this matter because they grew and matured at a time when the Nazis prohibited him from speaking and publishing. Noack elucidates the "meaning of Greek-Christian dogmatic theology from the view of the humanities"[40] especially by pointing to Origen, who lived and thought on the point of intersection between pagan and Christian thought.

> When the young Acton calls the writings of Origen 'delightful' ... there is in this a valuable hint regarding the final set of issues of his own spiritual state, and not only his own but that of the Catholic-Christian, and indeed of any study of humanities carried out from a Christian orientation. Because by venerating Origen's creative genius, Acton and Döllinger combine the recognition that the condemnation of Origen's system by the church (in AD 399 in Rome) was justified ... but at the same time we see the tying of the knot here of the eternal drama between Catholicism and freedom of conscience, which will keep recurring.

Then as now, the matter is the "harmony between 'science' and 'faith.'"[41]

According to Noack, Origen admittedly

> brought into balance various factors: cosmological and soteriological, what is and what should be. But he made far too sharp a distinction between faith and theology—speaking in one way to the people and in another to the scholars. For the first time we can hear the theme of the tension between the faith of the people and the faith of scholars within Christianity—a tension that never again fell silent. And an ethical problem is tied to this tension, for cosmological and purely philosophi-

---

[40] Noack, *Katholizität und Geistesfreiheit*, 179.

[41] Noack, *Katholizität und Geistesfreiheit*, 179–80. Cf. Acton, Add. Mss. 5528, p. 53, excerpted in *SW* 3:615: "Real science and Christianity cannot come into conflict."

cal interests in theology at times prevailed over soteriological interests in Origen.[42]

"Origen, the ablest writer" in early Christianity, "spoke with approval of conspiring for the destruction of all tyranny."[43] This comes from the mouth of Acton, the historian of ideas. The partial condemnation of Origen's philosophy of religion at the hand of the magisterium nevertheless received the wholehearted approval of Döllinger as well as Acton. Neither one saw this condemnation as an attempted act of paternalism toward thought. When it is a matter of theological questions, a final word is needed regarding the struggle of differing interpretations. Because the doctrine of papal infallibility (as understood by those advancing it and by many who supported it) involved political issues and not theological ones, Acton remained an unbending opponent of it. In political affairs it is paramount to rescue the principle of freedom. In scientific matters, on the other hand, it is different: here it is about rescuing the truth.[44] The revelation of truth fulfills itself in the conscience, when one sees it (as Acton did) as the voice of God and thus aligned to an ontology.

What then is the conscience? It is the verdict of the inner self of a person who is faced with a choice, because one can think and act in one way or another. Life in its tension—"the dialectic of spirit and fire [of God, whom people experience as a living spirit and consuming fire] shapes ... a person's spiritual self awareness in the verdict of one's conscience."[45] And yet the conscience as the *hēgemonikon* (authoritative leading) of the soul remains hard to comprehend, all the more so because Acton is certainly right when he says, "conscience is not absolutely infallible."[46] But as much as conscience distinguishes itself by giving counsel with final certainty to the one who heeds it (a certainty that is otherwise unattainable in any of the questions of theoretical knowledge), the conscience still does not provide unconditional

---

[42] Noack, *Katholizität und Geistesfreiheit*, 181.

[43] Acton, "The History of Freedom in Antiquity," in *SW* 1:27.

[44] Cf. Acton, Add. Mss. 4960, p. 61, excerpted in *SW* 3:650: "Gift of reasoning, of logical demonstration, moves truth forward by a constant pressure."

[45] Schockenhoff, *Zum Fest der Freiheit*, 251.

[46] Acton, Add. Mss. 5626, p. 15, excerpted in *SW* 3:502.

protection from error. This is why Acton adds that conscience "is the result of training."[47] Following one's conscience is something that needs to be practiced.[48]

All things considered, Acton sees an abyss between the *civitas Dei* and the *civitas terrena* that cannot be crossed. In his essay "The Roman Question," which was originally published in 1860 in his paper the *Rambler*, Acton makes an assessment that cannot be more matter-of-fact and harsh: "There is a wide divergence, an irreconcilable disagreement, between the political notions of the modern world and that which is essentially the system of the Catholic Church. It manifests itself particularly in their contradictory views of liberty, and of the functions of the civil power. The Catholic notion, defining liberty not as the power of doing what we like, but the right of being able to do what we ought, denies that general interests can supersede individual rights."[49] It is valuable to continue reading here, because a few lines further down Acton justifies his liberalism, which is critical of the state, as being the necessary result of this understanding of freedom and also happens to address the vast difference between the Continental idea of freedom[50]—often informed by principles of despotism and in this case completely contradictory to Catholicism's teaching on freedom—and that of the Anglo-Saxon world, which has its own idea of freedom.

Acton's rationale for freedom takes place in two steps: "Conscience a Basis of liberty. Therefore religion a basis of liberty."[51] The con-

---

[47] Acton, Add. Mss. 5626, p. 15, excerpted in *SW* 3:502.

[48] Cf. Acton to Mary Gladstone, March 31, 1883, in *SW* 3:503: "To develop and perfect and arm conscience is the greatest achievement of history, the chief business of every life, and the first agent therein is religion or what resembles religion."

[49] Acton, "The Roman Question," excerpted in *SW* 3:613. In light of this background one can better understand Acton's confession in his letter to John Henry Newman, dated June 4, 1861: "In the House [of Commons] I find that I am perfectly isolated, and without hopes of obtaining any influence for my principles. I am sure I can do better in another sphere" (*The Letters and Diaries of John Henry Newman*, ed. Charles Stephen Dessain and Francis J. McGrath, 32 vols. [London: T. Nelson, 1961–2008], 19:504).

[50] Acton, "The Roman Question," excerpted in *SW* 3:613.

[51] Acton, Add. Mss. 4960, p. 101, excerpted in *SW* 3:505.

science is the foundation and point of departure of his thinking. This conscience does not only demand practice—as already mentioned above—it also demands religion, that is, a dogmatic theology that is coherent and reasonable and that brings into a relationship what appears now and then as the demand of conscience. The state and politics have at their center but one task, to protect the freedom that people need to follow their conscience unopposed.

Thus the enemy of freedom is a type of politics that disputes this connection and either restricts the freedom that promotes the unfolding of the conscience or calls into question the very significance of the conscience. Acton calls this "political atheism."[52] The goal of this political atheism is to ground freedom on something other than the appeal to the sanctity of the conscience.

A liberal society for Acton is always also a secular society. He did not think it was necessary to position religion against liberalism and secularism. He was not willing, as a historian or politician, to recast society according to his religious convictions. Just the opposite: he believed that the abyss between religious and secular political dispositions could not be crossed. He had only one desire: to make it plainly evident to secular society that there is no other rationale for freedom but the conscience.

His interest in philosophers who held to a different view of freedom led, almost without exception, to the disclosure of flaws in their arguments, which become visible where other orientations that compete with freedom unfold at the expense of freedom. Therefore Acton says, "Liberty is the supreme law. Limited only by greater liberty."[53] This sentence finds its basis in reference to the conscience, which demands unconditional obedience.

In conclusion we must ask, are we today able to relate to this statement, that a liberal society that wants to last must be built on a religious foundation? A liberal society can only endure, according to Acton, when freedom is limited only by a higher measure of liberty. How far have we removed ourselves from this type of thinking, racking our brains day in and day out about the limits of freedom!

---

[52] Acton, Add. Mss. 5602, p. 45, excerpted in *SW* 3:500.

[53] Acton, Add. Mss. 5611, n. n., excerpted in *SW* 3:492.

Acton advises us not to contemplate the limits of freedom but rather the basis for freedom.

The superior position of the conscience—and of the concept of the conscience—is rooted in its significance as a hinge between two worlds: the conditional world and the unconditional world. In the contingency of all that is human, a window opens to the realm of the absolute, the divine, when we hear the inner voice of the conscience. There is an *a priori* quality in it that precedes all reflection.[54] Apart from that, human experiences are subject in every case to restrictive conditions; only the experience of the conscience is an unconditional, unlimited experience. When a human being listens to his conscience, he takes the plunge into a world in which what is valid has its validity independent of causes and limitations. The conscience is the place—the only place—of transition from that which is valid only under certain conditions to that which is valid under all circumstances. In this regard the conscience is the place in which the human being confesses himself to be a citizen of two worlds: totally rooted in the earthly conditions of existence yet simultaneously participating in the unconditional.

Contemporary constitutional thinking picks up on this meaning of the conscience. The freedom of the conscience, as it is protected by the German Constitution, according to article 4, paragraph 1, for example, "stands in a very close connection with the inner freedom of the human being that is protected under the name 'dignity.'"[55] All in all, the German Federal Constitutional Court has aligned itself with this evaluation (entirely in the sense of Acton) of the significance of the conscience as source of and rationale for a civil freedom that must be protected. What belongs to freedom of thought and of conscience, according to the opinion of this court, is "not only the

---

[54] Cf. Viktor E. Frankl, *The Unconscious God: Psychotherapy and Theology* (New York: Simon and Schuster, 1975), 33–34, regarding the "existential analysis of the conscience": The conscience is "prelogical. Just as there is a prescientific understanding and, ontologically even prior to it, a prelogical understanding of being, so there is likewise a premoral understanding of meaning, and this is conscience."

[55] Christoph Goos, *Innere Freiheit: Eine Rekonstruktion des grundgesetzlichen Würdebegriffs* (Göttingen: V&R unipress, 2011), 208.

(inner) freedom to believe or not to believe, but also the right of the individual to align his conduct according to the teachings of his faith and to act in accordance with his religious convictions."[56]

This ruling was handed down in 1972; since then, over forty years of societal development in the country have passed. Therefore it is necessary today to stress something else: what the court decided applies to the one with faith as well as to the one with no faith.[57] Everyone has the right both to decide and to act in accordance with their inner convictions, without interference. It goes without saying that this is easier said than done in specific cases. But in this conflict, which is inflamed by the specific case, a society's degree of liberty is demonstrated. One has to think and examine from time to time what exactly freedom means— and that means prioritizing the conscience.

One has to follow Acton, all things considered: "Conscience a Basis of liberty. Therefore religion a basis of liberty."[58] Liberalism and secularism, what in contemporary speech we call civil liberty, rest on the foundation of religion and thus on the foundation of the conviction that one's conscience is off-limits to others. This is what is meant when we speak about the sanctity of the conscience. Even so it must not be forgotten that the conscience's relationship to truth is what supplies the grounds for the freedom to follow it.[59] Whoever denies that there is an ontological foundation to the conscience can hardly uphold the demand for unconditional freedom of conscience. And exactly here lies a difficulty for today, because when many think about decision of the conscience, they all too often think of an opin-

---

[56] Federal Constitutional Court 33, 23 (28), quoted in Goos, *Innere Freiheit*, 62.

[57] An allusion to Henri de Lubac's dedication in *De la connaissance de Dieu* (Paris: Éditions du Témoignage chrétien, 1948): "A mes amis qui croient et à ceuse qui croient ne pas croire" [To my friends who believe and to those who believe they do not believe].

[58] Acton, Add. Mss. 4960, p. 101, excerpted in *SW* 3:505.

[59] Cf. Honnefelder, "Vernunft und Gewissen," in *Der Streit um das Gewissen*, 116: "The connection to truth, that constitutes the *obligation* of conscience demands at the same time the inviolability of *freedom* of conscience" (emphasis in original).

ion that merely reflects a momentary and subjective conviction, but not one that expresses a lasting objective standard.

By declaring that its telos is to protect the freedom of the conscience, the liberal society is itself grounded in the untouchability of the conscience, which is indisputable. It is only in this claim that the liberal society can recognize the ultimate ground of its liberality. Its liberality is thus rooted precisely where it asserts the claim to neutrality and secularity, namely, in a religious faith. This faith in turn is the starting point for the self-attestation of our society in its constitutional framework—by analogy to the self-attestation of its citizens to be unhindered in doing what they feel obligated to do according to their conscience. If this belief in the priority of freedom dwindles as other reasons for liberalism come to the fore, then freedom is downgraded to being just one goal among many. In that case it is logically necessary to weigh, case by case, which goal society wants to give greater weight to. In liberal democracies such decisions occur in parliaments and, thus, by majority vote. Then freedom faces a rocky road, robbed of its unconditional grounding and reduced to an object of deliberation—to an object of compromise, in other words. When this happens, freedom usually is tossed aside because other goals that are more important to a majority at the moment come to the fore. Acton saw through this process with a rare clarity. It is exactly here that the most profound reasoning is to be found behind Acton's admonition, reminiscent of Alexis de Tocqueville, about the danger of "absolute democracy"—the tyranny of the majority.

4

LORD ACTON ON THE HISTORIAN*

Josef L. Altholz

L ord Acton is rightly remembered as the historian of liberty in
the context of religion and conscience, and primarily applied
to politics and political thought. Acton's political views were formed
by his work and experience as a historian, his discovery of the historian's need for intellectual liberty, which led to his larger concern
for liberty in all spheres in which conscience might be involved.
Acton thought much and wrote a fair amount about the rights and
duties of the historian. This essay will be devoted to his thoughts on
the historian. I say "on the historian," not "on history," deliberately.
Acton, I will argue, was a moralist, and he thought about his subject in terms of the moral duties of those who study it. His thoughts
about his profession are relevant to the study of religion and liberty
because, for Acton, liberty of historical thought and writing was
founded on religious principles, the moral obligation of truthfulness,
and the sanctity of truth.

In the *Dictionary of National Biography*, where the opening of an
entry gives a descriptive term for the subject's occupation or area

---

*Originally given as the Lord Acton Lecture at the Acton Institute,
January 1996.

of importance, Acton is defined as "historian and moralist."[1] This is the only instance of the conjunction of these terms. Yet it is exactly right. Even the aphorisms that give Acton his current significance in political thought are essentially moralistic in a context of history. In rewriting his entry for the *New Dictionary of National Biography*, I again describe Acton as "historian and moralist."[2] This unique conjunction is nowhere better seen than in his thought about the historian.

Acton was typically Victorian in his devotion to the ideal of Truth (which he often wrote with a capital *T*). The most important virtue, he was to teach his children, was to tell the truth. Acton was also typically Victorian in his failure to recognize the two distinct things that are conflated in the word *Truth*. There is factual truth, that which actually is; and there is truthfulness, the moral condition or state of mind that seeks to describe facts honestly. Acton, the moralist, was primarily concerned with the moral quality of truthfulness. He assumed, perhaps naïvely, that if this were joined to proper methods of research it would lead to historical truth. This was to him the attractiveness of the discipline of history, which as he discovered it in the mid-nineteenth century had learned to discard its prejudices and to work objectively from valid original documentary sources, thereby becoming a true *Wissenschaft*, a word imperfectly translated as "science." To resist the conclusions of historical science was thus a sin against truth. What historians required was to be allowed to seek truth for its own sake, to operate freely by their own methods, independent of external authorities and without concern for the effects of their work. The truthful pursuit of truth required complete freedom of inquiry. So morality led to liberty, first in history.

---

[1] J. Neville Figgis, "Acton, John Emerich Edward Dalberg, first Baron Acton of Aldenham and eighth baronet (1834–1902)," in *Dictionary of National Biography Second Supplement*, vol. 1 (Oxford: Oxford University Press, 1912).

[2] Josef L. Altholz, "Acton, John Emerich Edward Dalberg, first Baron Acton (1834–1902)," in *Oxford Dictionary of National Biography*, ed. H. C. G. Matthew and Brian Harrison (Oxford: Oxford University Press, 2004), online ed., ed. David Cannadine, October 2009, http://www.oxforddnb.com/view/article/30329.

Acton's thought on these matters was formed in the early 1850s by his apprenticeship at Munich to Ignaz von Döllinger, the leading Catholic historian in Germany. It was a heady time for students of scientific history, a discipline largely shaped in German universities. Objectivity had been discovered as a virtue both necessary and useful, releasing the historian from the chains of partisanship and freeing him, in the phrase of the leading historian Ranke, to show "what actually happened" (*wie es eigentlich gewesen*). The critical method of examining sources produced new and sounder interpretations of historical authorities, and Ranke pioneered the study of basic original sources just at a time when many of the archives of Europe were being opened to scholars. Acton found himself Döllinger's fellow student in the new archival history. Döllinger, brought up in the older critical school, taking part in the free competition of Catholic and Protestant scholars, had an apologetic motive behind his objectivity, seeking to prove that Catholics could be as sound and objective as Protestants and thereby to disprove canards against his church. But scientific history won over the historian, and the historian triumphed over the priest: Döllinger, followed by Acton, discovered and exposed the failings of his church. In the late 1850s and early 1860s, Acton as a Catholic journalist in England and Döllinger as a Catholic historian in Germany were criticized for excessive freedom and objectivity in their criticisms of their church. The issue of intellectual freedom thus became personal to both men, in the form of freedom of historical scholarship against the authorities of the church. It was a papal attack on the freedom of scholarship asserted by Döllinger in 1863 that led Acton to close his journalistic career in 1864. His first struggle for liberty was thus on a religious ground, a struggle for freedom *within* religion for the scholarly conscience against ecclesiastical authority.

The first liberty for which Acton contended was intellectual liberty. It may seem odd that the historian of political liberty should have first confronted the church rather than the state, but in the latter nineteenth century Acton did not have to defend intellectual liberty against the state. Wilhelmian Germany might have been authoritarian but scrupulously respected academic freedom; the stodgy conservatism of Austria shielded the brilliant universities of Vienna and Prague; other countries, with Britain in the lead, allowed or even encouraged freedom of thought and the press. Only the authorities of the Roman

Catholic Church sought to impose control, and it was therefore those authorities that Acton had first to fight. In his general theory of liberty, Acton valued the corporate church, as he valued other corporate bodies, as a buffer between the state and the individual, but his early experience showed the need of a buffer between the individual and the institutional church, and he was even willing to call on the less autocratic state to perform that role. In 1870 he urged Gladstone to join in a general protest by the great powers to prevent the definition of papal infallibility. In 1871 he saw Döllinger excommunicated by the church but protected in his tenure at Munich by the fact that it was a state university. Acton was ready to defend liberty by any means against all threats.

This generalization of what had begun as a defense of intellectual liberty within the church took shape when Acton made his grand tour of European archives in the late 1860s. What these original sources showed was the "conventional mendacity" of Catholic historians, their practice of falsehood and suppression of truth to further the interests or reputation of the church. For one whose commitment to truth was integral to his religion, this perversion by religion of the moral obligation of the historian was fundamentally evil. What especially appalled Acton was that the particular facts suppressed by mendacious historians concerned the crimes committed by leading churchmen, including popes and saints, notably the sanctioning of killing in the interest of the church and the practice of persecution unto death. Acton's morality on this subject was as simple, perhaps simplistic, as his morality of truthfulness: killing is simply murder, the worst of crimes. Yet church authorities had practiced persecution; popes and saints had authorized the killing of heretics; theologians had justified such things as doctrine; and historians had either suppressed or excused these facts. Persecution was to become the touchstone of Acton's historical morality, raising his critique of his church from the ecclesiastical to the ethical plane. But it was not only a critique of the church. The state, especially the absolute monarchies, had engaged in persecution and political murder with no less vigor. So Acton's growing hatred of persecution merged into his long-standing hatred of absolutism, initially formed under the influence of Burke but now taking shape in the context of a particular concern as a historian.

This was a concern that differentiated Acton from Döllinger in their historical mentalities. It was a difference that Isaiah Berlin was to illustrate by the analogy of the hedgehog and the fox: the fox knows many little things, but the hedgehog knows one big thing. Döllinger, the veteran historian, knew all sorts of historians' lies and ecclesiastics' crimes, but he knew them singly. Coming to this knowledge relatively young and suddenly, Acton was able to generalize it into a system pervading history in general. In 1867 Pius IX canonized a notorious inquisitor, Pedro Arbués. To Döllinger this signified that the church had sanctified the principle of persecution, and he now found himself in ethical opposition to Rome. To Acton, already in ethical opposition, Arbués was just another part of the pattern, a mere illustration of the system of lies and murder.

Acton's judgment of the church throughout history was so severe as to make his opposition to one event, the definition of papal infallibility at Vatican I in 1870, less fundamental than it was to Döllinger. Acton agreed with Döllinger that the infallibilist position was dangerous as absolutism and was based on bad history. Döllinger opposed the dogma as essentially false and accepted excommunication rather than submit. Acton felt that the pre-1870 church had so many crimes on its record that the addition of one dogma could not tip the scales any further. If Rome was the true communion before 1870, it was the true communion still, despite its faults. In his reply in 1874 to Gladstone's attack on papal infallibility in its bearing on the civil allegiance of Catholics, Acton pointed out numerous cases in which church authorities had been guilty of political crimes without invoking papal infallibility; English Catholics had ignored papal commands in the past, and a newly defined dogma would not change their civil allegiance. He thus justified present-day Catholics by revealing the faults of the historical church. Acton used the occasion to make one last plea for the freedom of church history: "It would be well if men had never fallen into the error of suppressing truth and encouraging error for the better security of religion.... I should dishonour and betray the Church if I entertained a suspicion that the evidences of religion could be weakened or the authority of Councils sapped by a knowledge of the facts with which I have been dealing."[3] Acton's faith transcended history. The church taught a divine truth that could not be compromised by the actions of men, even popes and saints. The more Acton exposed the crimes of churchmen, the more he asserted his faith. So he did not spare the church he loved.

After the Vatican crisis was over, in the late 1870s, Acton formed his plans for what would have been his magnum opus, the *History of Liberty*, which has been called the greatest book never written. It is not quite true that it was never written. His lectures on the History of Freedom, delivered in 1877, provide a seventy-page prospectus for the larger work, a brilliant overview of the grand theme. His *Cambridge Lectures on Modern History* are animated throughout by his mature theory of the history of liberty, almost as if he had taken up the theme anew and brought it to completion under another guise. But the project as Acton had formulated it in the late 1870s was effectively aborted in the early 1880s, as I will explain shortly. That project, however, was a rather narrow one, covering only about 150 years, from the 1680s to 1830, with an English Whig theme, not the near-universal span of the History of Freedom lectures nor even the modern history of the Cambridge lectures. The notes for it, published in 1994 by George Watson, contain brilliant aphorisms but suggest that the connected narrative might have been disappointing. The greatest book never written may owe its greatness to the fact that it was never written.

What brought the *History of Liberty* project to a stop was the moral crisis brought on by Acton's break with Döllinger. This grew out of Acton's ideas of the moral function of the historian. The issue here was persecution, which Acton had long regarded as simply murder, by common consent the most heinous of crimes. Religious persecution, killing for the sake of the church, was worst of all. Precisely because the crime of persecution had its source in that which ought to be the source of morality, it was most to be condemned. Further, it was no private crime. It was pursued by public authority for a public end, thus corrupting the entire society. Worse still, persecution was justified by theorists, thereby being perpetuated as a doctrine for the future. The evil had been brought into the heart of the church; it was

---

[3] Acton to the editor of the *Times* in response to Gladstone, November 30, 1874, in *Correspondence*, 138.

in Acton's words "the fiend skulking behind the Crucifix."[4] Here Acton merged his morality and his history. He thought that morality and history shared a common "scientific" ground: murder could serve as an objective standard of evil in both. On this basic point, morality must be upheld by the historian. As a historian of ideas, Acton was most concerned with the idea of persecution. Worse than the actual murderer is the theorist who justifies murder, and the historian who defends or even fails to condemn either is no better. The historian must not be morally indifferent ("objective" in our current usage). He must be a judge, applying the moral standard as a canon of judgment, admitting no exceptions. He must indeed judge most harshly the best of men, those who ought to know better. So Acton criticized Catholics more than Protestants, clerics more than laymen, popes and saints most of all.

This ethical rigorism applied to history brought about a break with Döllinger. The incident that caused it seems slight compared with the absolute difference of principle that it revealed to Acton. In 1879 Döllinger prefaced a short letter to an uncritical obituary article on the French bishop Dupanloup. Acton regarded Dupanloup as a man who was ready to justify the worst abuses of the papacy and thus was no better than those who committed crimes in the name of the church. He was shocked to find that Döllinger did not agree with him. Döllinger refused to condemn men for their mere weaknesses, choosing to explain rather than to judge; Acton judged men readily, making no allowance for the morality of past times. What ensued from this affair was the revelation to Acton that even his friend and mentor did not share his ethical rigorism, that he was absolutely isolated in his fundamental position. The shock of this revelation paralyzed Acton's creative faculties for several years.

In the mid-1880s Acton returned to historical work, as part of a movement to create a historical profession in England, becoming one of the founders of the *English Historical Review*. When the editor, Mandell Creighton, an Anglican clergyman, invited Acton to review his own *History of the Papacy*, Acton produced a harsh review criticizing Creighton's failure to condemn the popes of the Reformation era.

---

[4] Acton to Lady Blennerhassett, n.d. [February 1879], in *Correspondence*, 56.

In the ensuing correspondence, in which incidentally Creighton had the better of the argument, Acton uttered his famous phrase about power tending to corrupt and absolute power corrupting absolutely. This is most commonly cited in a political context, as a condemnation of state absolutism, which Acton indeed abhorred. But in this instance his dictum was meant as a canon of historical criticism, a caution against the mitigation of judgment.

> I cannot accept your canon that we are to judge Pope and King unlike other men, with a favourable presumption that they did no wrong. If there is any presumption it is the other way against holders of power, increasing as the power increases. Historic responsibility has to make up for the want of legal responsibility. Power tends to corrupt and absolute power corrupts absolutely.... There is no worse heresy than that the office sanctifies the holder of it.... The inflexible integrity of the moral code is, to me, the secret of the authority, the dignity, the utility of history. If we may debase the currency for the sake of genius, or success, or rank, or reputation, we may debase it for the sake of a man's influence, of his religion, of his party, of the good cause which prospers by his credit and suffers by his disgrace. Then history ceases to be a science, an arbiter of controversy, a guide of the wanderer, the upholder of that moral standard which the powers of earth, and religion itself, tend constantly to depress.[5]

This was the most noble mission ever assigned to the historian, but it may have been the most impossible. For one thing, there was no consensus as to how the moral standard was to be applied. More important, professional history is the study not of text but of context. Historians are trained to place actions and events in the context of time and place, considerations that are fatal to an absolute morality that is timeless and universal. As Owen Chadwick put it, there is a tension between "historical understanding and moral conviction": "Moral judgment," which is "the essence of the *man*," "corrupts the

---

[5] Acton to Mandell Creighton, April 5, 1887, in *SW* 2:383–84.

historian.[6] The professionalization of the discipline of history meant that historians could not accept the moral role that Acton proposed for them. They were reduced from universal histories to monographs and from moral arbiters to a necessarily valueless objectivity. Yet Acton, isolated but admired, remained engaged with history and historians. He reaped his reward when in 1895 he was appointed Regius Professor of Modern History at Cambridge University, potentially the most influential position a historian can hold.

It is customary for Cambridge professors to begin their tenure with an inaugural lecture, and Acton seized the occasion to profess his historical creed. He concisely restated his theme of the history of liberty by defining "the Unity of Modern History" (the period since the Renaissance) as a constant "progress in the direction of organised and assured freedom," which he regarded as the work of Providence through history and discerned by historians.[7] Then Acton turned to the development of scientific history in the nineteenth century, under the influence of Ranke, whom he described as his "master," archivally researchful, critical of sources, and above all, impartial. Acton suggested the necessity and also the limitations of scientific history, "a discipline which every one of us does well to undergo, and perhaps also well to relinquish."[8] This led to his concluding section, asking himself if he had "any cardinal proposition, that might serve as his selected epigraph, as a last signal, perhaps even as a target."[9] His answer was to reassert his doctrine of the historian as moral judge: "I exhort you never to debase the moral currency or to lower the standard of rectitude, but to try others by the final maxim that governs your own lives, and to suffer no man and no cause to escape the undying penalty which history has the power to inflict on wrong," for "if we lower our standard in History, we cannot uphold it in Church or State."[10]

---

[6] See Owen Chadwick, "Acton and Butterfield," *Journal of Ecclesiastical History* 38, no. 3 (July 1987): 401, 402, 404.

[7] Acton, *LMH*, 11; *SW* 2:517.

[8] Acton, *LMH*, 18; *SW* 2:532.

[9] Acton, *LMH*, 23; *SW* 2:545.

[10] Acton, *LMH*, 24, 28; *SW* 2:546, 552.

This was a grand and noble ideal; it was expressed with an eloquence unusual for Acton; but it was also hopeless. Acton founded a school of history at Cambridge, but it was not a school of Actonian history, of which he was the first and only practitioner. Working historians then and since have settled for mere objectivity as the best they can achieve. Acton must have known that he was uttering a hopeless protest against the inexorable tendency of the historical profession he was helping to found. He had suggested that it was "a last signal, perhaps even ... a target"; and his great sentence of exhortation began with an acknowledgment that "the weight of opinion is against me."[11] Having uttered his protest, Acton spent the rest of his Cambridge career working with historians on their terms, accepting their limitations. His own lectures advanced his own themes, but the last great project of his life, the *Cambridge Modern History*, forced him to admit that objectivity (he preferred to say "impartiality") was the most that he could ask of his colleagues.

Acton's 1896 prospectus for the *Cambridge Modern History* envisioned the opportunity of "recording ... the fullness of the knowledge which the nineteenth century is about to bequeath," based upon critical research in archives, to be produced by a "division of labour" in which each chapter would be written by the English-speaking scholar most competent on the subject. But how could such a number of men achieve consistency of approach, or how could eminent writers be bound to one common theme? The only answer was to insist on absolute impartiality, the avoidance of any point of view. "We shall avoid the needless utterance of opinion, and the service of a cause. Contributors will understand that we are established, not under the meridian of Greenwich, but in longitude 30 West"—that is, not in one country but in the middle of the Atlantic Ocean.[12] Acton no doubt expected that the completed work (which he planned but did not live to publish) would manifest his theme of the unity of modern history as progress toward liberty, but this was to be accomplished by the organization of volumes and chapters, not by statements of position.

---

[11] Acton, *LMH*, 24; *SW* 2:546.

[12] Acton, *Longitude 30 West: A Confidential Report to the Syndics of the Cambridge University Press* (Cambridge: Cambridge University Press, 1969), here quoted from *SW* 3:676.

This emphasis on neutrality was the main theme of Acton's letter to the contributors, sent out in 1898. "Our scheme requires that nothing shall reveal the country, the religion, or the party to which the writers belong. It is essential not only on the ground that impartiality is the character of legitimate history, but because the work is carried out by men acting together for no other object than the increase of accurate knowledge. The disclosure of personal views would lead to such confusion that all unity of design would disappear."[13] In effect, Acton acknowledged that he was leading a team that could be held together by nothing other than impartiality; even he could arrange no design other than what would naturally emerge from the structure as a whole. For one who had so ample a vision of history and so high a conception of the moral function of the historian, mere objectivity must have seemed like a lowering of the standard, but it was eminently practical, representing the only standard that could be achieved by actual historians.

Acton's ideal of the historian as judge, as the upholder of the moral standard, is the most noble ideal ever proposed for the historian; and it is an ideal that has been rejected, perhaps with grudging respect, by all historians, including myself. We workaday historians can seek no more than to attain a high level of mediocrity, and we can have no higher ideal than Acton's second choice, impartiality or objectivity. In this sense, as also in his relative lack of publications, Acton was somewhat of a failure as a historian. Yet he remains relevant to historians, not as a model but as a challenge. If Acton stands on the far right of historians, demanding something more than objectivity, there is a significant far left that would do away with objectivity altogether, and many others who would sharply modify that already moderate standard. Their critique is based upon the valid observation that it is difficult or even impossible for historians to meet the standard of objectivity, that they will always be affected by their time, their place, their creed, perhaps even their gender. This can be constructively applied as a call to historians to acknowledge their limitations and make the best of them. But it has also been applied as a justification for abandoning any standard, for elevating the historian above the

---

[13] Acton, *LMH*, 316.

historical record, denying that there is any objective factuality, and allowing an individual historian in effect to create his or her own past—the historical equivalent of deconstructionism and other postmodern tendencies in literary studies. To this, Acton in his isolation serves at least as a counterpoise, a countervailing force allowing the center to hold. For the historian of today, Acton serves not as an example but as a counter-example, providing a standard that we do not follow but that enables us at least to reject its direct opposite.

There is much of failure in Acton's career, whether as liberal Catholic, as politician, or as historian. In the 1970s there was some criticism of the continuing study of such a failure, and the late Sir Geoffrey Elton even proposed a moratorium on Acton studies. Yet in these centennial years Acton studies is a prospering small industry, which suggests that there are some failures that are more interesting and even valuable than mere success could be. Had Acton been a success either by his standards or by ours, he would have been a less instructive subject for our study. The spectacle of such a man doomed to failure not by the limitations of his thought but by his own too exacting standards is at once a source of humility and of inspiration. Failure is especially worthy of study when it reveals the fierce integrity of Acton's devotion to conscience, to truth, and to liberty.

5

LORD ACTON, THEORETICIAN OF POLITICS

Justification and Abuse of Political, Ecclesiastical, and Societal Power*

Rudolf Uertz

Translated by Victoria Huizinga

For hundreds of years Christianity has promoted the existing political and cultural powers and, above all, conservative ideas and principles, due in no small part to the legitimation of political sovereignty that comes from reasoning grounded in a theology based on biblical revelation.[1] Since the 1980s the study of politics and current

---

*Originally published in German as "Lord Acton, ein Theoretiker der Politik. Rechtfertigung und Missbrauch politischer, kirchlicher und gesellschaftlicher Macht," in *Glaube, Gewissen, Freiheit. Lord Acton und die religiösen Grundlagen der liberalen Gesellschaft*, ed. Christoph Böhr, Philipp W. Hildmann, and Johann Christian Koecke (Wiesbaden: Springer, 2015), 180–97.

[1] For centuries the classic passage for Christian and ecclesiastical thought on the state was Romans 13:1–7, which begins: "Let every person be subject to the governing authorities. For there is no authority except from God, and those that exist have been instituted by God. Therefore he who resists the authorities resists what God has appointed." The natural-law interpretation, which reflects historical-contingent and socio-ethical conditions, as well as illegitimate political rule, finds its high point in medieval Scholasticism, especially in Albert the Great and Thomas Aquinas in the thirteenth century. Baroque Scholasticism—Francisco Vittoria, Francisco Suarez, and others in the sixteenth century—and neo-Scholasticism draw on high Scholasticism but

events as well as the study of fundamentalism have confirmed the tight relationship between religions—including Christianity—and both conservative political and societal ideas in particular. Analyses of the history of theology and of ideas, however, show that the Christian religion and ethics can be combined with many different political movements and ideas. Today, the Protestant churches—of which the Anglican is the largest denomination—and the Roman Catholic Church affirm human rights, democracy, and the rule of law as the basis of modern statehood.

The connection between the Christian religion and liberal political thought is prominently evident in the life and writings of the English historian John Emerich Edward Dalberg-Acton. From 1859 to 1866 Acton was a member of the British House of Commons and was a promoter of the politics of the English liberal prime minister William Ewart Gladstone. In 1869 Acton became the first Catholic to enter the House of Lords since the separation of the Anglican church from the papal church in 1534. This honor for the English aristocrat was surely a belated satisfaction, given the fact that his desire to study in England had been rejected by three universities, among them Cambridge, on the grounds that he was a Catholic.[2] This rejection caused Acton to study in Edinburgh, Scotland, as well as at the University of Munich, where he studied history and theology under the well-known church historian Ignaz von Döllinger. Also influential on Acton was the historian Leopold von Ranke. In 1872 Acton received an honorary doctorate in philosophy from the University of Munich and in 1876 he was admitted into the Bavarian Academy of Sciences as a nonresident member. In 1880 he was made a fellow

---

modify it considerably. Cf. Rudolph Uertz, *Vom Gottesrecht zum Menschenrecht: das katholische Staatsdenken in Deutschland von der Französischen Revolution bis zum II. Vatikanischen Konzil (1789–1965)* (Paderborn: Schöningh, 2005), 236–37.

[2] Cf. Johannes B. Müller, "Lord John Emerich Edward Dalberg-Acton," in *Lexikon des Konservatismus*, ed. Caspar von Schrenck-Notzing (Graz: L. Stocker, 1996), 13ff. As is well known, F. A. Hayek originally wanted to name the Mont Pelerin Society (founded in April 1947) the "Acton-Tocqueville Society," but in light of the protests from Ludwig von Mises and Frank Knight against naming it after two Roman Catholic aristocrats, it was agreed that the liberal society should be named after the venue in Switzerland.

of All Souls College in Oxford, and in 1891 he was made Regius Professor of Modern History at Cambridge.

The purpose of the following discussion is to outline Acton's political theory and ethics; his understanding of the relationship between church and state in the light of his activities during the First Vatican Council in Rome (1869–70) as it relates to the dogma of papal infallibility; and his approach to democracy, constitutionalism, and social order.

RELIGION AND POLITICS IN THE THOUGHT OF LORD ACTON

The political ethics of Lord Acton is primarily built on two foundations. The first is Greek philosophy, in the tradition of Socrates and the Stoics. In this line of thought, which is also indebted to transcendental thinking, Acton constructs the most important distinctions for his understanding of the relationship between law and injustice, and between good and evil. According to Socratic and Stoic philosophy, human beings were given reason and conscience to make that determination. Endowed with this ability humans have a solid basis for thinking about order that must follow ethical standards. But for Acton it is the Christian religion that brings the crucial element for the "development of the freedom of conscience, since it provides what Greek philosophy, for all its Socratic and Stoic wisdom, cannot provide: the distinction between state and society, between state and church."[3]

The natural endowment of humans with reason and conscience meant much for the "emancipation of human conduct,"[4] but nothing had been done with that yet. "But when Christ said: 'Render unto Caesar the things that are Caesar's, and unto God the things that are God's,' those words, spoken on His last visit to the Temple, three days before His death, gave to the civil power, under the protection of conscience, a sacredness it had never enjoyed, and bounds it had

---

[3] Ulrich Noack, *Politik als Sicherung der Freiheit. Nach den Schriften von John Dalberg-Acton dem Historiker der Freiheit 1834–1902* (Frankfurt am Main: G. Schulte-Bulmke, 1947), 133.

[4] Noack, *Politik als Sicherung der Freiheit*, 133.

never acknowledged; and they were the repudiation of absolutism and the inauguration of freedom. For our Lord not only delivered the precept, but created the force to execute it."[5]

One can easily see that Acton's ethical-personal position is built on a synthesis of philosophical and theological reasons. This approach unmistakably differentiates the English historian from the neo-Scholastic natural-law theory that had been expanding since the mid-nineteenth century. This theory started in Italy after Pope Leo XIII's encyclical *Aeterni patris* in 1879 met with official ecclesiastical approval, and functioned until the start of the 1960s as the official political and social-ethical guideline of the church. It considerably shaped and influenced the politics and programs of the German Centre Party as well as other Christian democratic parties in central Europe.

Acton's interpretation of society, politics, and law differed clearly from the specific natural-law interpretation of the official ecclesiastical teaching on state and society, which was based on the pope's state and social encyclicals, dictated an interpretative frame for Christian moral teaching, and sanctioned any deviation from the norms the church had decreed. The ecclesiastical-cultural and political atmosphere that was coupled with the emerging neo-Scholasticism, which came into being under Pius XI's papacy (1846–78), had strong integral features. Moral theology and Catholic teaching on the state at this time took for themselves the right, through the instrument of *potestas indirecta*—the indirect power of the pope, or, as the case may be, the teaching of the church in worldly matters—to dictate societal, cultural, and political-ethical guidelines too. They were meant to guide Catholics in their everyday lives of marriage, family, society, state, and cultural matters. In this way it was possible for the neo-Scholastic teaching and praxis of the church to infiltrate the Catholic parties—the Centre Party, Christian people's parties, unions, and others—and have a significance influence.[6]

This form of centralization of clerical power and authority, as well as guidance of laypeople by clerics and the teaching of the church,

---

[5] Acton, "The History of Freedom in Antiquity," in *SW* 1:28; cf. Matthew 22:21 and Mark 12:17.

[6] Cf. Carl Ulitzka, "Soll der Klerus die Führung in der Öffentlichkeit übernehmen?," *Die Seelsorge* 6 (1928/1929): 321ff.

experienced its greatest excess under the papacy of Pope Pius IX. With his encyclical *Quanta cura* and the *Syllabus* of 1864, which was primarily a judgment against both liberal and moderate liberal middle class ideas, the pope declared principles and rules that must have been greatly offensive to a liberal thinker such as Lord Acton.[7] Informed by his religious and philosophical understanding of moral conscience, Acton advocated decisively for the separation of church and state, as well as the differentiation between religion and politics, whereas Pius IX condemned these positions in his *Syllabus*. It is important here to note that the excesses in the papacy and among the Roman Curia had to do with Rome's attempts to continue to secure the worldly reign of the pope over a church-state (756–1870) and to declare this as a necessary condition for ecclesiastical freedom and pastoral care.[8]

This kind of close connection of the human conscience and Christian morality with ecclesiastical-pastoral standards, along with mechanisms of interpretation and control, were foreign to Acton's imagination. His ethical-personal position is rooted to a considerable degree in English Common Sense thought, a much more free and pragmatic interpretation of social-philosophical and natural-law principles than was aimed at by the neo-Scholastic system of thought that consistently guided French- and German-speaking Catholics. Influenced by his studies with Ignaz von Döllinger and the close relationship he cultivated with this well-known church historian, Acton was well prepared in his role as critic of the papal teaching on faith and morality.

---

[7] For the English text of the encyclical *Quanta cura*, see *The Papal Encyclicals*, vol. 1, *1740–1878*, ed. Claudia Carlen (Wilmington, NC: The Pierian Press, 1990), 381–86. For the English text of the *Syllabus*, see Henry Denzinger, ed., *The Sources of Catholic Dogma*, trans. Roy J. Deferrari (St. Louis: B. Herder, 1957), 433–42.

[8] Cf. Uertz, *Vom Gottesrecht zum Menschenrecht*, 193–94.

Liberal Ethics and the Rejection
of State Absolutism

This blending of religion and politics, church and state, and church dogma and civil life, which marked the Catholicism of the second half of the nineteenth century under the papacy of Pius IX, deeply contradicted Lord Acton's thoughts about freedom and his sense of conscience, which he claimed for himself precisely as a believing Catholic, without becoming a heretic. Acton's understanding of law and state is influenced by the Anglo-Saxon understanding of law, which differs significantly from the continental European tradition, which was shaped by Roman law. The characteristics of Common Sense Philosophy, as well as the corresponding common-law school of thought will be mentioned here briefly: Common law is a case law, a casuistic law, which orients itself to precedents, which were ruled by courts.[9] Common law does not operate by abstract principles, as the constitutional continental European legal system does, but rather builds upon decisions of the past that have proven viable. Because there are no time limits to the binding applicability of precedents, this case law is more conservative than the statutory law that is known by other European legal cultures. Having said that, the Anglo-Saxon law also knows a competing, dynamic legal culture, the so-called equity law or equity jurisprudence, which, in the end, comes down not so much to the traditional argument as to a reflected and wise situational decision.

Thus one can see significant correlations in the legal thought of Acton and Edmund Burke, who is considered more of a conservative by continental European observers.[10] But Acton is more flexible and liberal than Burke. And he does not share the extreme positions of

---

[9] Cf. Theo Stammen, *Der Rechtsstaat: Idee und Wirklichkeit in Deutschland*, 4th ed. (Munich: Bayerische Landeszentrale für Politische Bildungsarbeit, 1972), 41–42; René David, *Einführung in die grossen Rechtssysteme der Gegenwart*, trans. Günther Grasmann (Munich: Beck, 1966), 15–16, 323–24.

[10] Cf. Edmund Burke, *Reflections on the Revolution in France* [1790], in *Select Works of Edmund Burke*, vol. 2 (repr., Indianapolis: Liberty Fund, 1999), 85–476; Karl Graf von Ballestrem, "Burke," in *Klassiker des politischen Denkens*, 2 vols., 5th ed., ed. Hans Maier, Heinz Rausch, and Horst Denzer (Munich: Beck, 1987), 2:118ff.; Manfred Henningsen, "Burke," in *Vom Nationalstaat zum Empire*.

a populist and radically democratic style that attempts to impose a
new order in the state and society. Acton rejects every form of state
absolutism as simply immoral. In a letter to Richard Simpson he says,
"I understand by political science the development of the maxim
suum cuique in the relations of the state with other states, corpora-
tions and individuals."[11] Burke's resistance to a radical change of the
British constitution in the sense intended by Parisian intellectuals is
grounded in his belief that the constitution grew up on English soil
and therefore fundamentally included civil rights and liberties, which
the French could only import. Acton, on the other hand, emphasizes
more strongly that the essence of freedom and political ethics is not
to be found in outward forms and demands but rather in the living
conscience, so that the sphere of constitutional life is not based on
dead letters of edicts and regulations, but rather on the living thoughts
of people.

HISTORICAL LAW AND THE NEW LAW

Acton identified the first principle of legislation to be that it "should
grow in harmony with the people,"[12] that it is based on customs as well
as on prescriptions, and that it identifies with the national character
and life. What Acton outright rejects are the codes that are forcefully
imposed on a people, such as those that were introduced in continental European states in the fifteenth century with the Roman law.
This system, administered by "legists, jurists, bureaucrats," proceeds
"downwards," so that the people are not the ones who administer
the law, which of course grows out of the morality and customs of
the people.[13] An orderly system, accordingly, has to grow, and naturally it also can be changed in response to developments in culture,
technology, and society, but this change has to occur cautiously.
Thus Acton, just like Burke, rejects the voluntaristic theory, at least

---

Englisches politisches Denken im 18. und 19. Jahrhundert, ed. Manfred Henningsen
(Munich: List, 1970), 43ff., esp. 48–49.

[11] Acton to Richard Simpson, May 7, 1860, in *CLARS* 2:58–60.

[12] Acton to Simpson, January 5, 1862, in *CLARS* 2:251.

[13] Acton to Simpson, January 5, 1862, in *CLARS* 2:251.

its radical-democratic version. But how does this fit with Acton's later position? His German biographer Ulrich Noack writes:

> A generation later he celebrates the American War of Independance as "the abstract revolution in its purest and most perfect shape," as "the most notable circumstances that people have seen," and says about the Americans: "On the principle of subversion, they are building the greatest political system in the history of humanity."[14]

One can detect in Acton that his judgments are based on the history of legal systems. Noack makes a point of emphasizing that these are very different from traditionalistic, or legitimist, arguments. For Acton, radical changes, no matter whether they come "from above" or "from below," are always immoral and destructive, because they place the past and future in opposition to one another and place exclusive value on the one or the other. But when it comes to what is inescapable, such as legal facts that are operative and cannot be changed anymore, British constitutional thought is not willfully obstructive, but demonstrates a realistic-pragmatic view. Acton as a young man, according to Noack, is "much more conservative than the older Acton; one could say that in the beginning he was a Whig but later became a devoted liberal. His views of tradition and revolution, and therefore his view of the essence of a state's institutions, receive a different coloring. But the contrast is not a sharp one; the transition is a smooth one."[15] Noack tries here to get to the bottom of Acton's thoughts of law and state. But it is not necessary to distinguish between the young and older Acton, because Acton remains faithful to British constitutional thought throughout his life. It is perhaps less his personal development that is significant here; rather, his thinking is tied to the events in the American colonies, which forced Acton, just as much as Burke, to accept the inevitability of the increasing political and administrative independence of the American colonies as a fact of law and to legitimize them constitutionally.

It should be noted in this context that Catholic teaching on state and law, which was put in effect by the papacy of Leo XIII (1878–1903),

---

[14] Noack, *Politik als Sicherung der Freiheit*, 144.

[15] Noack, *Politik als Sicherung der Freiheit*, 144.

combines its specifically Thomist–natural law ideas with historical legal thought to a considerable degree. This becomes clear in Pope Leo XIII's attitude toward the French Republic. The pope advises the French in his encyclical *Au milieu des sollicitudes* (1892), after he had diagnosed the irretrievability of the monarchical order, to "Acceptez la république!" Catholic teaching on the state, as well as historical legal thought in general, does not allow for a change of system from monarchy to a republican or democratic order. Similarly, Scholastic teaching on the state proceeds from the assumption that when a new order prevails, even if by revolution, this new order can and must be accepted as legitimate as long as it (according to the legal-ethical grounds of Catholic teaching) does not contradict the common good. Thus, the Catholic teaching on the common good can in principle justify a democratic order in place of a monarchic one. Problematic for the Catholic teaching on the state is the separation or differentiation between morality and law. In this regard the ecclesiastical teaching differs from the secular historical thinking on law, whose English version was represented by Lord Acton. While Acton systematically differentiates between ethics and law, neo-Scholasticism's clerical teaching on the state views the law as nothing more than the outskirts of ethics and morality.[16] Because of this, it is difficult, from the aspect of Catholic legal theory, to acknowledge the positive right of the state as a legitimate right, of which Acton naturally disapproved.

It is important to observe, in terms of political and legal theory, that the historical legal thought as represented in England—and to some degree on the Continent—relies, with regard to the history of ideas, on the classical Thomist model.[17] To what else but vested rights should

---

[16] Cf. Ernst-Wolfgang Böckenförde, introduction to *Erklärung über die Religionsfreiheit: Zweites Vatikanisches Ökumenisches Konzil* (Münster: Aschendorff, 1968), 16–17.

[17] Cf. Leo Strauss, *Natural Right and History* (Chicago: The University of Chicago Press, 1953), 296. It may be surprising that Burke—as also incidentally the Scholastic teaching on the state—goes back to a classical or Thomistic model, which then of course was also true of Lord Acton. However, common law, which also takes up traditional elements of Scholastic natural-law theory, differs from its neo-Scholastic version. This becomes evident in the *Magna Carta* (1215). In this respect, continental European law emphasizes more the legal idea of freedom—"free person"—whereas the English system

monarchies such as England and the papal state refer? To what else but the "historical law"? In other words, in English constitutional and legal thought, the poles of persistence and change, conservatism and liberalism, are much closer than in continental European thought, which since the nineteenth century has been influenced much more by the rationalistic theory of natural law coming out of France. This differentiation must always be taken into consideration when characterizing Acton's theory of society and state and this theory's qualification as "liberal."[18]

THE VATICAN COUNCIL AND THE DOCTRINE OF PAPAL INFALLIBILITY

Acton remains faithful to his principles of socio-ethical and legal theory in his attitude toward ultramontanism and the ecclesiastical-curial movement right up to the assertion of the doctrine of papal infallibility at the First Vatican Council (1869–70). Acton, who after his studies in Munich under Döllinger (1850–54) worked as publisher of philosophical-theological and historical writings and served from 1859 to 1865 as a liberal member of the House of Commons, was appointed as peer to the British House of Lords by the English Prime Minister William Ewart Gladstone on December 11, 1869. Acton's appointment happened only three days after the opening of the First Vatican Council in Rome. This temporal connection was not entirely coincidental. Acton was one of the most prominent critics of the decisions of this council.

On July 18, 1870, in the fourth session, the constitution *Pastor aeternus*, which included the infallibility doctrine, was officially adopted, with 522 voting in favor and only 2 opposed. Acton did not have an official assignment to serve as an observer of the council for the English government, but he stayed in close contact with Prime Minister Gladstone via the English embassy's diplomatic courier service. Just like other European statesmen, Gladstone had a keen interest in the doctrinal decisions of the council. As member of the

emphasizes the legal norms and procedure. Cf. Stammen, *Der Rechtsstaat*, 46–47.

[18] Cf. Roland Hill, *Lord Acton* (New Haven: Yale University Press, 2000), 74.

House of Lords, Acton had a diplomatic status. This status, along with his good connections to the Curia and the main leaders of the supporters, as well as to the critics of the doctrine of papal infallibility among the participants of the council and publicists, meant that Acton was well informed regarding the deliberations concerning the constitution *Pastor aeternus* and the intentions of its originators and opponents. From Rome he also informed Döllinger, who under the pseudonym "Janus" frequently published articles in the *Augsburger Allgemeine Zeitung* about the internal affairs of the preparations and consultations in the council.[19]

For the Catholic Church and for the majority of European states— England, France, Bavaria, Prussia, and others—the doctrine of papal infallibility and its background were a political issue of the greatest significance. It was feared that the dogmatic constitution of the infallibility of the pope would include far-reaching political and socio-ethical powers for the Roman pontifex, so it was not an unwarranted concern that the council would decree new norms that could impact civil obedience and fiduciary duties toward the ruler. There were good reasons to assume that the decisions of the council by means of extensive interpretation of the Catholic teaching on morality and faith would lead to tensions between Catholics and Protestants in states where the population was confessionally mixed. Similar worries were voiced by the Bavarian government.[20] Take, for example, the president of the council, curial cardinal Karl-August von Reisach—appointed by the pope—the former bishop of Eichstätt and archbishop of Munich and

---

[19] Cf. Johann Joseph Ignaz von Döllinger, *Der Papst und das Concil* (Leipzig: E. F. Steinacker, 1869); ET: *The Pope and the Council* (Boston: Roberts Brothers, 1870). The substance of this book originally appeared in 1869 as a series of articles in the *Augsburger Allgemeine Zeitung* under the nom de plume "Janus."

[20] Döllinger was excommunicated by the archbishop of Munich because he did not submit to the doctrine of infallibility. On the occasion of the four hundredth anniversary of the Ludwig Maximilian University in the summer of 1872, honorary doctorates were given to Lord Acton, William Ewart Gladstone, and John Stuart Mill, among others. "But the central figure in these events was the rector of the University, Dr. Döllinger. In deliberate response to Rome's excommunication, the highest grade of the Bavarian Order of Merit was bestowed on him by the Bavarian prime minister" (Hill, *Lord Acton*, 249).

101

Freising. After the announcement of the council, immediately after the publication of the *Syllabus* on December 6, 1864, he declared in an opinion that a new council was necessary, arguing that "the last council, that of Trent, had not expressly refuted the fundamental error of the reformers, namely their denial of the hierarchical structure of the Church and her authority to teach unerringly. This omission had created some uncertainty even within the Church herself."[21]

The preparations for the council stood therefore in a close connection (in both time and content) with the condemnations of the liberal principles of modern statehood as expressed in the *Syllabus*. Among other things, this pertained to human rights and rights to freedom as well as to the separation of state and church. Because of this, and not least owing to the activities of the Curia and the accompanying material that appeared (especially the distribution of the Jesuit publication *Civiltà Cattolica*), there was fear that the pope would interpret his power of teaching so broadly that—as Acton feared—not only future statements of the pope but also obvious erroneous judgments and heresies of former popes would fall subject to the claim of papal infallibility.

POLITICAL AND ECCLESIASTICAL RAMIFICATIONS OF THE COUNCIL

Contrary to fears, the Vatican Council, with its ceremonial adoption of the constitution *Pastor aeternus*, in fact did not establish such a far reaching definition of papal authority, because it tied authoritative papal statements of doctrine to specific conditions.[22] This did not

---

[21] Hubert Jedin, *Ecumenical Councils of the Catholic Church: An Historical Outline*, trans. Ernest Graf (New York: Herder and Herder, 1960), 191.

[22] See *Dogmatic Constitution I on the Church of Christ*, in Denzinger, ed., *The Sources of Catholic Dogma*, 457:

> The Roman Pontiff, when he speaks *ex cathedra*, that is, when carrying out the duty of the pastor and teacher of all Christians in accord with his supreme apostolic authority he explains a doctrine of faith or morals to be held by the universal Church, through the divine assistance promised him in blessed Peter, operates with that infallibility with which the divine Redeemer wished that His church be instructed in defining doctrine on faith and morals; and so such definitions of the Roman Pontiff from himself, but not from the

change the fact, however, that the doctrine of infallibility could with-stand neither strictly biblical-exegetical methods nor the merely reve-latory theological statements in the New Testament. On the contrary, it seemed preposterous, in light of the historically grown fullness of power and authority of the papacy, to posit this as an entire system of belief and of law. The papacy is historically based on a primacy of honor. The doctrine of papal infallibility made the claim of papal powers excessive.[23]

In this context it is easy to apply Acton's most famous statement to papal powers too: "Power tends to corrupt and absolute power cor-rupts absolutely."[24] The argument relating to the inopportuneness of the dogmatic definition, not however the infallibility in and of itself, was represented by many European and American bishops. Among them were many of the most highly educated theologians at the coun-cil, such as Bishop Wilhelm Emmanuel von Ketteler of Mainz, who, like the other Inopportunists among the bishops, left before the synod had concluded but submitted to papal infallibility later. It is true to say that the broad opposition of bishops, priests, and laity, especially from northern and middle European countries, could claim that their opposition had prevented the definition of broader claims to papal power, as had been discussed by the ecclesiastical press.

The relationship between Acton and his former teacher Döllinger is also remarkable in this context. Both agreed not only that the defi-nition of papal infallibility was inopportune for political-cultural and ecclesial-political reasons, but also "that the teaching is wrong."[25] Acton saw the doctrine of infallibility as a result of a spiritual climate that contradicted the theological-ethical doctrine of the freedom of conscience, and so the doctrine of infallibility cannot be given the

---

consensus of the Church, are unalterable. But if anyone presumes to contradict this definition of Ours, which may God forbid: let him be anathema.

[23] Cf. August Hasler, *How the Pope Became Infallible: Pius IX and the Politics of Persuasion*, trans. Peter Heinegg (Garden City, NY: Doubleday, 1981).

[24] Acton to Mandell Creighton, April 5, 1887, in *SW* 2:383.

[25] Ulrich Noack, "Liberale Ideen auf dem Ersten Vatikanischen Konzil. Lord Acton in Rom 1869/70," *Historischer Zeitschrift* 205 (1967): 81ff. (quote on p. 85).

highest claim to truth even by the authoritative decision of a pope. This means that the doctrine's claim to truth is based on an erroneous opinion and a consequential wrong decision that cannot be rectified. As Roland Hill comments, "Acton's disillusion with the Church was in a sense greater than Döllinger's but also less, for Acton at least entertained the thought that the dogma of Infallibility might one day be 'explained away' or, as Catholics of the Vatican II generation might say, placed in its theological context, whereas Döllinger hoped for a retraction, which Rome would never make. Acton and Döllinger were agreed that there existed among Catholics an attitude towards religion that was immoral."[26] Döllinger was an extraordinary church historian but not as well-versed in systematic theology; according to Acton, he had never sufficiently considered the religious-ethical and psychological climate in which the doctrine of infallibility was able to come into being in the absence of enough mechanisms that could have prevented the worst from happening. So it certainly is a paradox that Acton—who according to Noack was so greatly influenced by Döllinger's teaching in terms of his assessment of the inopportunity of the doctrine of papal infallibility—and Döllinger were so estranged from each other on precisely this issue; at the end of the day the two views were irreconcilable.

The argument between Acton and his former teacher erupted in, of all places, the context of an obituary for Félix Antoine Philibert Dupanloup (1802–78), bishop of Orléans and member of the French Academy, that Döllinger had coauthored under his nom de plume. Even though Dupanloup was one of the Inopportunists among the participants of the council, in a discussion Dupanloup once had shown appreciation for the *Syllabus*, which condemned the liberal

---

[26] Hill, *Lord Acton*, 319–20. The fact is that the Second Vatican Council modified the doctrine of infallibility of 1870 by putting it into a different context. Walter Kasper writes in *Publik* (December 12, 1969), here quoted from Hans Küng, *Infallible? An Inquiry*, trans. Edward Quinn (Garden City, NY: Doubleday, 1971), 199: "The overcoming of ecclesiastical triumphalism by Vatican II affects also the Church's understanding of truth and demands a new and more profound interpretation of the concept of infallibility, which is so open to misunderstanding. This concept belongs more than any other to the still unmastered past of Vatican I."

theory of state and society, and he had been praised by the pope specifically for that.

Acton thought it incomprehensible that Döllinger could have not investigated the immoral attitude of Roman Catholicism toward religion, namely, that there were unmistakable connections between the condemnation of liberal principles by Pius IX in the *Syllabus* of 1864 and the doctrine of infallibility of 1870. Döllinger did not appreciate that the encyclical *Quanta cura* and its condemnations of freedom of religion, conscience, and opinion provided the intellectual breeding ground in which the doctrine of infallibility could thrive. Among the conditions by which it came into being was not only a religious irrationalism but also, along with this, a belief in miracles that displaced reasoning and that was especially prevalent among the Catholics in southern Europe, among whom were also members of Jesuit orders who belonged to the advisors of the council and, furthermore, cardinals, curial bishops, and even the pope himself.[27]

Acton discusses in a letter to Döllinger the immoral attitude of Catholics toward religion, which he says consists in the belief that

> sin ceases to be sin if it is committed for the purposes of the Church. Theft is not theft, lies are not lies, murder is not murder, if they are sanctioned by religious interests or authorities.... We are therefore dealing not with heretics or skeptics but with liars, thieves, and murderers—be it in actuality or potentially. Thus we have a much worse enemy than Protestantism, because Protestantism is compatible with the strictest morality and because this view poisons the fount of truth, the elixir of the church.[28]

---

[27] Cf. Hill, *Lord Acton*, 318–19. The intellectual-religious climate in which the council preparations took place becomes evident in a speech given by the archbishop of Messina, Luigi Natoli, in which he said that Saint Peter himself preached infallibility in Sicily. After all, the Madonna had confirmed this deputation (cf. Hill, *Lord Acton*, 221). Regarding the belief in miracles in Rome in the nineteenth century and its shady side, cf. Hubert Wolf, *Die Nonnen von Sant'Ambrogio. Eine wahre Geschichte* (Munich: Beck, 2013).

[28] Acton to Döllinger, n.d. (ca. 1879–80), here quoted from Ignaz von Döllinger, *Briefwechsel*, vol. 3, *Ignaz von Döllinger—Lord Acton 1871–1890*, ed. Victor Conzemius (Munich: Beck, 1971), 212–13.

Acton's liberal stance toward integrity, which does not differentiate between a position of moral theology and one of philosophical ethics, demonstrates its extensive dimensions here. Acton even accepts a break from Döllinger, his teacher and friend of many years, which adds a further personal and tragic note to the history of the impact of the doctrine of infallibility.

Democracy and Social Order

Acton recognizes the tremendous power that can proceed from the Christian teaching on conscience for human beings and for the commonwealth in a liberal order. The basis for his free and democratic understanding of people and society is the conscience, or the conscientiousness of the human being. However, along with the opportunities that freedom presents to humans, there are also certain connected dangers, such as the abuse of power in the hands of individuals, of institutions, and of collectives, as well as revolutions and riots. The right order, according to the theory of a mixed constitution, which English and Catholic thought have in common, therefore should preserve the middle ground between unrestricted democracy and abstract idealistic absolutism. That means, first, that the order of the state cannot exclusively be the product of deliberate creation by human beings and citizens, but rather—just like law—grows with the passing of time and, second, that the state receives its authority precisely from the fact that the state as legislator is "heteronomous." The state stands over society but is also bound to law and justice.[29]

Noack points out the different evaluations that Acton gave regarding revolution throughout his life, and he characterizes the younger Acton as more conservative than the older one. Whereas Acton condemned revolution in early statements because, as he argued, a nation cannot "cast off its history, reject its traditions ... and commence a new political existence,"[30] he was enthusiastic about the American Revolution and wars for independence: these were "abstract revolu-

---

[29] Noack, *Politik als Sicherung der Freiheit*, 152–53.

[30] Acton, review of *Irish History*, by Goldwin Smith, *Rambler*, n.s., 6 (January 1862): 190–220, here quoted from *SW* 2:76; cf. Noack, *Politik als Sicherung der Freiheit*, 142.

tion in its purest and most perfect shape," and he said that Americans, "on the principle of subversion ... are building the greatest political system in the history of humanity," and he welcomed it as "the most notable circumstances that people have seen."[31]

Noack's evaluation refers us back to the above-mentioned theory of the state. The French Revolution is a radical overthrow, whereas the American Revolution is a secession and the creation of a completely new order. For historical legal thought this is a special challenge. Something new, or even a new order, cannot be justified merely on the basis of tradition. The American order is voluntaristic and grounded on the social contract theory and is in this sense a new legal creation. In fact, however, Acton evaluates the American Revolution (and the deliberate-artificial element of human work and energy) to be a deeply ethical-anthropological element: human beings are co-creators of the order of a community, and depending on the situation, the duty to act, informed by the conscience, can be greater or smaller. Regarding the American constitution, Acton positively evaluates, not least, "the system of a federalist government ... which astonishingly increases the national power, and which nonetheless respects local freedom and authorities," which corresponds to the "principle of equality."[32] In this sense moralistic-political decisions can never be static and deduced from general principles. Indeed Acton sees the societal and political balance in the America of his time as troubled, because Americans could not lean "on the ideas of former generations" as the Europeans could.[33]

It is not a contradiction when Acton, who approved of the American Revolution, rejects a radical democracy just as much as an absolute monarchy. "Both republics and monarchies are either absolute or *organic*, that is, they are either governed by laws, in other words constitutionally, or by means of will, which (because it is the basis for laws and cannot therefore be its object) is despotic. Only in the way they *grow*, in the direction toward which they gravitate, are democracy and monarchy directly antithetical."[34] The criterion that Acton uses

---

[31] As quoted in Noack, *Politik als Sicherung der Freiheit*, 144.

[32] Noack, *Politik als Sicherung der Freiheit*, 154.

[33] Noack, *Politik als Sicherung der Freiheit*, 155.

[34] Noack, *Politik als Sicherung der Freiheit*, 151 (emphasis in original).

to assess these two different orders of democracy and constitutional monarchy are the civil rights, as well as the rules and provisions, that correspond best to the area of accountability of the citizens. These are the constitutional institutions and the balance of powers inside the political community. In the *Rambler*, a paper that Acton published from 1858 to 1862, in "Political Causes of the American Revolution," he wrote,

> [Democracy and monarchy] differ, therefore, not only in direction, but in the principle of their development. The organization of a constitutional monarchy is the work of opposing powers, interests, and opinions, by which the monarch is deprived of his exclusive authority, and the throne is surrounded with, and guarded by, political institutions.... Hence monarchy grows more free, in obedience to the laws of its existence, whilst democracy becomes more arbitrary. The people is induced less easily than the king to abdicate the plenitude of its power, because it has not only the right of might on its side, but that which comes from possession, and the absence of a prior claimant.[35]

With his pointed theory of personal ethics, Acton clearly recognized that progress was moving toward the enlargement and expansion of a liberal-democratic order, for which he undoubtedly had much sympathy given his personal disposition. On the other side, shaped in his thinking by the English experience, he recognizes that a constitutional monarchy with its balance between throne and the forces of the opposition—privileged classes and their parliamentary representation—presents a more favorable system of state and legal order than a liberal-democratic system, since Acton (who saw this in the development of America) could not quite tell where the path of that system would lead. This shows itself in Acton's perplexity regarding the tension between democracy and the sovereignty of the people, majority rule and the rights of minorities, as well as between

---

[35] "Political Causes of the American Revolution," *Rambler*, n.s. (3rd ser.) 5 (May 1861), here quoted from *SW* 1:217.

the unitarian system and federalism—the "most difficult chapter" in Acton's system.[36]

Unlike Burke, Acton recognizes the social dimensions of further progress; besides the democratic and constitutional principles, that means the necessity of standards and regulations for a socio-political welfare state, for which Acton entertained much greater sympathies than Burke. However, Acton was not yet able to delineate future societal and socio-political structural orders. His outline of the potential problems in this regard, however, goes quite far for a political thinker who saw himself as a defender of individualism against public authority based on the Stoics' teaching of equality, fraternity, and humanity—even though his prognosis here for the future too is quite general. Acton analyzes the differences between freedom and democracy by reference to the antagonisms between the South and the North in the American union. He admittedly hopes that the doctrine of equality will also include in the future the concept of responsibility, but he fears, with good reasons, that in America there is a fight against a true sovereignty of the people. Regarding this matter Acton refers to economics as well as to the problem of property and possessions for freedom and democracy.

He leans on the theories of the English socio-political thinkers John Lilburne (1614–57) and James Harrington (1611–77). Their theory of the necessity of the balance of property made them the first to have recognize the "real conditions for democracy," and in many regards, to have "seen as clearly and as far as we see today."[37] Acton calls the teaching of these early social reformers "as important as the invention of printing, or the discovery of the circulation of the blood."[38] It is the recognition that power follows property. According to Acton, this is what Lilburne and Harrington believed, even though they were lacking empirical evidence. Acton, however, proceeds from this theory as if it were a law. "The cleavage between the political and the social democrat, which has become so great a fact in modern

---

[36] Noack, *Politik als Sicherung der Freiheit*, 152.

[37] Acton, "Sir Erskine May's *Democracy in Europe*," in *SW* 1:72; Noack, *Politik als Sicherung der Freiheit*, 158.

[38] Acton, "Sir Erskine May's *Democracy in Europe*," in *SW* 1:72; Noack, *Politik als Sicherung der Freiheit*, 159.

society," complains Acton, "was scarcely perceived."[39] Political democracy, which relies on the equality of civic rights, is the foundation for constitutionalism. Acton discards social democracy, but he concedes that "legal equality must strive towards balance of property," since power follows property "as by a law of nature" and the government obtains "its form from the dominant powers of society." It is obvious that Acton recognizes the fundamental dilemma of the contemporary-modern social state and its tension between "teaching on freedom and law."[40]

Noack states that Acton sees clearly "that the terms of civil freedom and social order bring no social service to the masses of the people."[41] As Acton writes, what the masses mean by freedom is "that the strong hand that heretofore has formed great States, protected religions, and defended the independence of nations, shall help them by preserving life, and endowing it for them with some, at least, of the things men live for.... That is also its purpose and its strength. And against this threatening power the weapons that struck down other despots do not avail."[42] Acton criticizes the divine rights of big landowners, which the revolution of 1688 put in place of the divine right of the king, and in this regard he characterizes John Locke as "thin, lacking in energy and impoverished, since his 'notion of liberty involves nothing more spiritual than the security of property.'"[43]

Noack comments that "the goal of liberal social politics," expressed in a programmatic and formulaic way, is, in Acton's words, "independence of labour and the security of property; to make the rich safe against envy, and the poor against oppression."[44] Again, Noack summarizes:

---

[39] Acton, *LFR*, 58.

[40] Noack, *Politik als Sicherung der Freiheit*, 159.

[41] Noack, *Politik als Sicherung der Freiheit*, 159.

[42] Acton, "Sir Erskine May's *Democracy in Europe*," in *SW* 1:81; Noack, *Politik als Sicherung der Freiheit*, 159.

[43] Noack, *Politik als Sicherung der Freiheit*, 160; Acton, "The History of Freedom in Christianity," in *SW* 1:47.

[44] Noack, *Politik als Sicherung der Freiheit*, 161; Acton, "The History of Freedom in Antiquity," in *SW* 1:12.

A sense of justice and empathy flow into each other here and are in the depth of his heart a matter of conscience borne by the religious person. To him, ignoring suffering is as bad as a crime, pure and simple. Just as he sees political justice as a matter of his religion, so too, he sees ignoring suffering as not just a sin before God but also a crime before people. Every honorable politician has a duty to punish publicly those who commit this crime. "We are bound ... to make the rude workman understand and share our indignation."[45]

CONCLUSION

The program that Acton championed could have derived from Pope Leo XIII's 1891 social encyclical *Rerum Novarum*. Acton basically appreciated the papacy, saw it as a unifying office and absolutely necessary, and never ignored the social context of Christian ethics. That is why he surely could have had no fundamental misgivings toward the papal teaching on social reform and its theory of property, which, contrary to some proponents of the more radical liberal camp, did not deserve to be labeled "socialistic." However, Acton was miles ahead of the papal teaching on the state with his liberal and constitutional theory, which included civil rights and rule of law. He essentially already represented a view that much later was taught by the Second Vatican Council's (1962–65) pastoral constitution *Gaudium et spes* and the declaration on freedom of religion in *Dignitatis humanae*, which made possible the ecclesiastical convergence toward human rights as well as liberal and constitutional ideas on order—ideas that already had circulated for some time within political and social Catholicism, as well as in Protestantism.

Acton's liberal-Catholic conviction about the conscience, which so inspired his opposition against the doctrine of papal infallibility and against the exaltation of spiritual and political power, finds clear expression in the famous witticism of Cardinal John Henry Newman, who was critically linked to his compatriot Acton. In Newman's letter

---

[45] Noack, *Politik als Sicherung der Freiheit*, 161; Acton to Mary Gladstone, April 24, 1881, in *Letters of Lord Acton to Mary, Daughter of the Right Hon. W. E. Gladstone*, ed. Herbert Paul (London: George Allen, 1904), 96.

to the Duke of Norfolk, he says, "Certainly, if I am obliged to bring religion into after-dinner toasts, (which indeed does not seem quite the thing) I shall drink,—to the Pope, if you please,—still, to Conscience first, and to the Pope afterwards."[46]

---

[46]John Henry Newman, *A Letter Addressed to His Grace the Duke of Norfolk on Occasion of Mr. Gladstone's Recent Expostulation* (New York: The Catholic Publication Society, 1875), 86.

6

QUEST FOR LIBERTY

America in Acton's Thought*

Stephen J. Tonsor

John Emerich Edward Dalberg Acton, as many people know, was
born on January 10, 1834. What is less commonly known is that
he was born not in England as becomes a proper English Lord, but
in Naples. The fact that he was born in the Palazoo Acton all'chiaja
in Naples is not without significance, nor is the fact that he died and
was buried in Tergensee, just south of Munich in Bavaria; for surely
aside from Prince Albert, Acton must have been the most un-English
of any prominent Englishman in the nineteenth century.

Lord Acton's grandfather, Sir John Francis Acton, whose name
"Johnny" Acton bore, had been an eighteenth-century English soldier
of fortune on a grand scale and had become "General Acton" and
prime minister of the Kingdom of the Two Sicilies. Ferdinand, King
of Naples, was a dullard and a buffoon who spent his time hunting
and amused himself by playing the hurdy-gurdy. His queen, Maria
Carolina, daughter of Maria Theresa of Austria and sister of the ill-
fated Marie Antoinette, had an eye both for power and powerful
men. Sir John Acton struck her fancy and rumor had it that John
Acton became her paramour. It was unsubstantiated rumor, however,

---

*Originally given as the inaugural Lord Acton Lecture at the Acton
Institute, January 1993.

for John Acton's steely nature knew enough not to mix the pursuit of power with the pursuit of pleasure. Together John Acton and Maria Carolina ruled the Kingdom of the Two Sicilies, ensuring its survival through the French Revolutionary and Napoleonic period. Our Lord Acton did not approve of his grandfather, and regarded the Neapolitan inheritance as "blood money." It is only fair to say that in all likelihood General John Acton would not have approved of his grandson, for he was an eighteenth century authoritarian who had nothing but contempt for liberty.

Those who would like to explore the Neapolitan world into which our Lord Acton was born in 1834 can not do better than read the magnificent novel by Giuseppe di Lampedusa, *The Leopard*, translated from the Italian by Archibald Colquhoun.[1]

Lord Acton's paternal uncle was a saintly cardinal, promoted to that position in 1842 when he was only thirty-nine by Gregory XVI. He died in 1847 in the Jesuit house in Naples. His name, Charles Edward Januarius, reveals the Neapolitan Acton connections. Harold Acton has given us a vibrant picture of the activities of General John Acton in *The Bourbons of Naples, 1734–1825*.[2]

Yes, it's an unlikely beginning for the historian of liberty and the passionate friend of the United States. His mother, moreover, brought an ancestry which was perhaps even less inclined to a devotion to freedom. Acton's mother was the daughter of the Duke of Dalberg. The Dalbergs were Electors of the Holy Roman Emperors, and in the imperial coronation ceremony at Frankfurt, a herald sounded a trumpet at the beginning of the coronation rite and called out, "Is there a Dalberg present?" at which point a Dalberg stood and identified himself and the ceremony was then able to proceed. Lord Acton's paternal grandmother belonged to a great Rhineland family. When Lord Acton's mother died in 1860 he inherited the Dalberg schloss at Herrnsheim in the Rhineland. In 1865 Acton married his cousin, the Countess Marie Ann Arco-Valley, a marriage which reinforced his German, in this case, Bavarian connections. Add to these bonds of birth and marriage the fact that Acton studied for six years at the University of Munich and it becomes clear that Acton's

---

[1] New York: Pantheon, 1960.
[2] London: Methnen, 1956.

Englishness was extremely attenuated. Acton was, in fact, a member of the Continental imperial aristocracy compared to which the Whig aristocracy which dominated nineteenth-century England (so brilliantly depicted in the Palliser novels of Antony Trollope) were the merest upstarts.

Still, Acton had Whig connections. When Lord Acton was three his father died, and in 1840, when Acton was six, his mother married Lord Leveson, later the Second Earl Granville, one of the great Whig magnates of the nineteenth century. Lord Leveson's uncle was the Duke of Devonshire, one of the wealthiest men in England in the nineteenth century. In short, Acton moved in circles characterized by wealth, power, and privilege; never mind that he did not ride and shoot and that his relationship to his stepfather was cool.

How, having been reared in such an atmosphere, are we to explain Acton's passionate commitment to liberty and his intense interest in and high estimate of the American experiment? In 1901, the year before his death, in his last lecture at Cambridge University, Acton concludes, "and yet, by the development of the principle of Federalism, [America] has produced a community more powerful, more prosperous, more intelligent, and more free than any other which the world has seen."[3]

It is the contention of this lecture that if we understand the development of Acton's attitude towards the United States we will find ourselves in possession of the key to Acton's thought in general.

Acton placed liberty in the forefront of all goods, moral and political. Many people are aware that the great uncompleted project of his life was the writing of a history of freedom. He saw the evolution of liberty as the work of Providence, as the consequence, as he put it, of Christ's being "risen on the world." Achieved liberty is the fulfillment of the divine plan. It is for this reason above all others that Acton so valued the American experiment.

Liberty, however, is seen as the end of history, achieved only in the fullness of time and only as a consequence of a long developmental process. Liberty, personal and political, could not come into existence until the way had been prepared for it by the development of conscience. Almost as important to Acton's thinking as tracing the

---

[3] Acton, *LMH*, 314; *SW* 1:197.

history of freedom was his effort to describe the growth of the idea of conscience. In the 60,000 volumes of his personal library he searched for the historical stages in the development of the idea of conscience. It was not an easy task and I might add it is a task which has been all but abandoned by philosophers and intellectual historians in our own day. Acton saw clearly that liberty was predicated on the existence of conscience. But what was conscience? What were the powerful arguments against the existence of conscience? How did the idea of conscience develop historically? Should the promptings of conscience always be obeyed? Could the conscience err? Was there a universal voice of conscience or was the conscience of each man a unique and independent authority? How did conscience manifest itself in politics? These are some of the problems with which Acton wrestled. Is it any wonder that he did not write his history of freedom?

The autonomy of conscience was, Acton tells us, recognized by Socrates and the Greeks. As he notes in his Additional Manuscripts, the word *conscience* occurs in the New Testament thirty-two times.[4] The Stoics believed that the voice of God dwells in our souls and that we must obey this voice. But Saint Thomas Aquinas is the source of the modern idea of conscience. Acton wrote in an extended note, "S. Thomas. As to penal laws, he went with his generation. For half a century when he wrote, not a voice had been raised for toleration. He strengthened a view which could hardly be stranger. But in respect of conscience he innovated. He went farther than all his time in proclaiming its authority. This was peculiarly his own idea—set out by him, and gifted with power, in time to overcome the other."[5] Acton further observed, "Conscience depends on, or is parallel with clear notions of ethics. Obscure ethics indicate imperfect conscience. Therefore obscure ethics imply imperfect liberty. For liberty comes not with any ethical system, but with a very developed one."[6]

Not until the seventeenth century was conscience grounded in a universal natural law. In his essay (1877), "The History of Freedom in Christianity" Acton wrote:

---

[4] Add. Mss. 4901, p. 66.

[5] Add. Mss. 4901.

[6] Add. Mss. 5395.

The French philosopher Charron was one of the men least demoralised by party spirit, and least blinded by zeal for a cause. In a passage almost literally taken from St. Thomas, he describes our subordination under a law of nature, to which all legislation must conform; and he ascertains it not by the light of revealed religion, but by the voice of universal reason, through which God enlightens the consciences of men. Upon this foundation Grotius drew the lines of real political science. In gathering the materials of international law, he had to go beyond national treaties and denominational interests for a principle embracing all mankind.[7]

Having established the primacy of conscience and rooted it in a universal natural law, Acton was ready to explore its political instantiation. He found that intersection of conscience, liberty, and politics in America.

As early as 1858 Acton had observed in an essay which appeared in his journal, the *Rambler,*

> The Christian notion of conscience imperatively demands a corresponding measure of personal liberty. The feeling of duty and responsibility to God is the only arbiter of a Christian's actions. With this no human authority can be permitted to interfere. We are bound to extend to the utmost, and to guard from every encroachment, the sphere in which we can act in obedience to the sole voice of conscience, regardless of any other consideration.[8]

Acton repeatedly noted that the Protestant Reformation and the wars of religion led to the establishment of absolutism rather than toleration and freedom. Royal power and bureaucratic administration, whether Catholic or Protestant, was substituted for the imperatives of conscience. Established churches used the power of the state to coerce the consciences of the subject. The Puritan revolution in England appealed to the higher law of conscience but then sank

---

[7] Acton, "The History of Freedom in Christianity," in *SW* 1:42.

[8] Acton, "Political Thoughts on the Church," *Rambler* n.s. (2nd ser.) 11 (January 1859): 30–49, here quoted from *SW* 3:29.

back into intolerance and repression. It was the sectarians, at first in England and then in America who justified religious nonconformity by an appeal to conscience.

In one manuscript, Acton wrote: "The theory of conscience was full grown. It had assumed in one of the sects, a very peculiar shape: the doctrine of inner light. The Quakers not originally liberals. But the inner light struggled vigorously for freedom. In the very days in which the theory of conscience reached its extreme terms, Penn proclaimed conscience as the teaching of his sect. And it became the basis of Pennsylvania—Voltaire's best government."[9] He added in another manuscript, "Conscience understood in this way supplied a new basis for freedom. It carried further the range of Whiggism. The deeper Quakers perceived the consequences, Penn drew the consequences in the Constitution of Pennsylvania. It was the standard of a new party and a new world."[10]

But not only the Protestant sects insisted on freedom of conscience and obedience to a higher law; Roman Catholics in Maryland pointed the way to the new world of freedom. In an essay, "The Protestant Theory of Persecution," published in the *Rambler* in March, 1862, Acton wrote:

At the same time when this involuntary change occurred [Anglican persecution under the Stuarts] the sects that caused it were the bitterest enemies of the toleration they demanded. In the same age the Puritans and the Catholics sought a refuge beyond the Atlantic from the persecution which they suffered together under the Stuarts. Flying for the same reason, and from the same oppression, they were enabled respectively to carry out their own views in the colonies which they founded in Massachusetts and Maryland, and the history of those two States exhibits faithfully the contrast between the two Churches. The Catholic emigrants established, for the first time in modern history, a government in which religion was free, and with it the germ of that religious liberty which now prevails in America. The Puritans, on the other hand, revived with greater severity the penal laws of the mother country. In

---

[9] Add. Mss. 4901, p. 355.
[10] Add. Mss. 4960, p. 299.

the process of time the liberty of conscience in the Catholic colony was forcibly abolished by the neighboring Protestants of Virginia; while on the borders of Massachusetts the new State of Rhode Island was formed by a party of fugitives from the intolerance of their fellow-colonists.[11]

In every case the appeal was to conscience, a conscience which defied the laws of man in order to obey the law of God. It was but a step from an appeal to liberty in religion to an appeal to liberty in politics. The appeal to the higher law made by the framers of the Declaration of Independence was only a more abstract and universal conception of liberty than the appeal to conscience made in the name of religion. Acton noted, "America started with the habit of abstract ideas. Rhode Island, Pennsylvania. It came to them from religion and the Puritan struggle. So they went beyond conservation of national rights. The rights of man grew out of English toleration. It was the link between tradition and abstraction."[12]

In his Cambridge University lecture (1901) on the American Revolution, Acton put the revolutionary shift from rights based on the fact that the colonists were Englishmen to rights based on a universal appeal to a higher law in this way:

> Then James Otis spoke, and lifted the question to a different level, in one of the memorable speeches in political history. Assuming, but not admitting, that the Boston custom-house officers were acting legally, and within the statute, then, he said, the statute was wrong. Their action might be authorised by parliament; but if so, parliament had exceeded its authority, like Charles with his shipmoney, and James with the dispensing power. There are principles which override precedents. The laws of England may be a very good thing, but there is such a thing as a higher law.[13]

---

[11] Acton, "The Protestant Theory of Persecution," *Rambler* n.s. 6 (March 1862): 318–51, here quoted from *SW* 2:131.

[12] Add. Mss. 4897, p. 130.

[13] Acton, *LMH*, 307; *SW* 1:191.

Acton argued with great force that England's colonial rule in America had been one of the mildest and most beneficent colonial regimes in history. Americans were not rebelling against oppression. The American course was justified solely on the basis of our appeal to a higher law, justified solely by an appeal to the rights of political conscience. These were arguments Acton understood, approved, and applauded.

The foundation of the American republic was, Acton rightly understood, not completed with the successful termination of the American Revolution. The American Revolution created a political society in which the unchecked will of the people was paramount, state governments in which the tyranny of the majority would, sooner or later lead to anarchy. The second great act of the founding, the making of the Constitution, was a conservative act which made the creation of a republic possible. The creation of the Constitution had two great objects in view, the prevention of the tyranny of the majority and the dispersion of centralized power. The framers of the Constitution achieved these objectives not through the enunciation of any new principles but by compromising contending tendencies and forces. The structure of the Constitution was like the structure of a medieval cathedral in which countervailing forces were employed in such a way as to hold the whole structure aloft. None of the great questions were resolved: states rights, federal power, the tariff, slavery. American federalism, which Acton reckoned one of the great inventions of the age, was based upon compromise rather than principle. From the beginning this structure of republican liberty threatened to collapse. In spite of their great achievement, Acton viewed the work of the founders as incomplete and the Constitution as an imperfect instrument.

It is my considered judgment that Acton was the most knowledgeable foreign observer of American affairs in the nineteenth century. As a very young man he had made a trip to the United States and had traveled widely, but the mature Acton's knowledge of America was based upon books rather than direct personal experience. No American, with the exception of Henry Adams, who was nearly his exact contemporary, knew American history more thoroughly than Acton. It is a pity that American historians so rarely read him.

They do not read him, I am convinced, because Acton espoused the Confederate cause in the Civil War, a struggle which Acton called "the Second American Revolution." In May of 1861 Acton published an enormously long essay in his journal, the *Rambler*, entitled, "Political Causes of the American Revolution." "The American Revolution" is Acton's designation for the Civil War. William Gladstone, later British prime minister, read Acton's essay, and it became the most determinative element in Gladstone's thought toward the warring American states. Had not Charles Francis Adams, the father of Henry Adams and US Ambassador to the court of Saint James, exerted his diplomatic talents to the utmost, Gladstone would probably have secured British intervention on the Confederate behalf.

Acton's reasons for his pro-Southern stance were well taken. In 1860 the great federative polities of Europe and North America were all under attack. Nationalism, centralization, and bureaucratic administration were dissolving and destroying the Germanic Confederation, the Austrian Empire, the patchwork of Italian states, and the United States of America. For Acton the retreat from states' rights and federalism in the United States was the most important and catastrophic of these developments.

In a letter to Robert E. Lee written in November of 1866 after the surrender at Appomattox, Acton states clearly his reasons for his sympathy for the Southern cause. He wrote the defeated Lee:

> Without presuming to decide the purely legal question, on which it seems evident to me from Madison's and Hamilton's papers that the Fathers of the Constitution were not agreed, I saw in State Rights the only availing check upon the absolutism of the sovereign will, and secession filled me with hope, not as the destruction but as the redemption of Democracy. The institutions of your Republic have not exercised on the old world the salutary and liberating influence which ought to have belonged to them, by reason of those defects and abuses of principle which the Confederate Constitution was expressly and wisely calculated to remedy. I believed that the example of that great Reform would have blessed all the races of mankind by establishing true freedom purged of the native dangers and disorders of Republics. Therefore I deemed that you were fighting the battles of our liberty, our progress, and our civilization; and I mourn for the stake

which was lost at Richmond more deeply than I rejoice over
that which was saved at Waterloo.[14]

Let there be no mistake about it: Acton was no defender or partisan of the institution of slavery. He abominated it as the very antithesis of the freedom which he saw as the supreme value of historical
development and the very work of Providence. Still, Acton was no
Northern abolitionist, and he saw slavery in the context of historical, religious, and ethical development; an institution rooted in the
ideas and circumstances of a particular era in time. It strikes one as
odd that Acton, who was an ethical absolutist, should, in the case of
slavery, have been a moral relativist.

Perhaps Acton's attitudes were the consequence of a hierarchy of
values in which absolute freedom is the end and final value contingent
upon the possession of other values. Clearly the threat to freedom
from centralized governmental absolutism, the tyranny of the majority, bureaucratic administration, democracy, and socialism were all
greater in Acton's estimate than the threat to freedom from slavery in
1860. It is only in this light that Acton's ambivalent attitudes toward
slavery in the Southern states of the United States can be explained.
That Acton shared this view with many others in Europe and America
should not come as a surprise to us.

Was Acton mistaken? Were his political fears like his religious
fears in the First Vatican Council of 1869–1870 exaggerated and
groundless? The victory of centralization, governmental absolutism,
the tyranny of the majority and bureaucracy were less complete in
1865 than Acton imagined they would be. Still, they remain the great
threat to freedom in our own day and they have grown in importance
and power since Acton's day. Statism is no less inimical to freedom
than are democracy and socialism. We should not delude ourselves
that because socialism has been defeated the enemies of freedom
have been routed. In these matters Acton's concerns must prove to
be our concerns.

In this brief discussion I have attempted to demonstrate that
Lord Acton's fascination with the United States provides us with an
insight into Acton's ethical and political philosophy. His concern with

---

[14] Acton to Robert E. Lee, November 4, 1866, in *SW* 1:363.

America was not one concern among many in a wide-ranging and expansive intellectual natural law and discerned by conscience. He believed this law higher than the power of churches or states, and he taught that the providence of God progressively enlarges human freedom and the ability to perform those acts which conscience dictates. These are the essential concerns of any Republican regime, America included.

In 1889 in a review of James, Lord Bryce's *The American Commonwealth* in the *English Historical Review*, Acton summed up the American accomplishment:

> Those who deem Washington and Hamilton honest can apply the term to few European statesmen. Their example presents a thorn, not a cushion, and threatens all existing political forms, with the doubtful exception of the federal constitution of 1874. It teaches that men ought to be in arms even against a remote and constructive danger to their freedom; that even if the cloud is no bigger than a man's hand, it is their right and duty to stake the national existence, to sacrifice lives and fortunes, to cover the country with a lake of blood, to shatter crowns and sceptres and fling parliaments into the sea. On this principle of subversion they erected their commonwealth, and by its virtue lifted the world out of its orbit and assigned a new course to history. Here or nowhere we have the broken chain, the rejected past, precedent and statute superseded by unwritten law, sons wiser than their fathers, ideas rooted in the future, reason cutting as clean as Atropos.[15]

---

[15] Acton, review of *The American Commonwealth*, by James Bryce, *English Historical Review* 4 (1889): 388–96, here quoted from *SW* 1:404.

7

LORD ACTON ON REVOLUTION*

Russell Kirk

O n the face of the matter, it may seem an insane conjunction to link with the name of John Emerich Edward Dalberg Acton, First Baron Acton, the revolutions of the past three centuries. Acton was a man of archives and books, sometimes called the most erudite scholar of his century. Born to great estate, he was the near kinsman of cardinals, cabinet ministers, and dukes. By station and residence he was protected against the violent events of his time. At his great country house of Aldenham in Shropshire, at his Bavarian estate of Herrnsheim near Worms, at his father's Neapolitan palace, or at his Tegernsee retreat, he saw nothing of social disorder or the rough side of life; unlike many young Englishmen of his station, he had no acquaintance with military life.

Indeed, his only encounter with the nationalist and socialist violence of the nineteenth century occurred at Rome in 1870, when Italian troops occupied the city while Acton was a hostile observer there of the proceedings of the Vatican Council. Yet Acton repeatedly commends revolution in his notes, literary fragments, and correspondence; five of his major essays and reviews are concerned directly with revolution, as is one of his two completed volumes of lectures, *Lectures on*

---

*Originally given as the Lord Acton Lecture at the Acton Institute, January 1994.

the French Revolution, published after his death. Gertrude Himmelfarb, in her biography of this great scholar, *Lord Acton: A Study in Conscience and Politics*, goes so far as to entitle one section of her eighth chapter "The Philosopher as Revolutionist."[1] So it may be worthwhile to trace the reflections of this eminent Liberal, friend of Gladstone, on those upheavals we call revolutions.

Now sometimes, in employing the word *revolution*, Acton merely means a revolution in the history of ideas, his chosen discipline; in the realm of thought, as in the political realm, he endeavored to recognize both the need for continuity and the necessity, at certain times, for an eruption of the new.

But also he sanctioned certain violent political revolutions that had occurred in the seventeenth, eighteenth, and nineteenth centuries—the Puritan Revolution, the English Revolution (of 1688), two American Revolutions (did you not know that two such occurred?), and even the French Revolution to some degree.

This tolerating of revolution occurred during the latter part of his life. The revolutions—or rather, the risings—of 1830 in the Continent had occurred four years before his birth at Naples; he had been a schoolboy at Oscott during the socialist and nationalist outbreaks of 1848; as he grew to manhood, made a journey to the United States in 1853, and presently studied with Dr. Döllinger, he became suspicious of democratic movements and hostile toward nationalism. He was greatly shocked by the atrocities of the Parisian Communards, who murdered the Archbishop of Paris on the barricades in 1871; Acton instructed his children to pray daily for the soul of the good Archbishop Darboy. Through studying with Döllinger, and through his own historical and political reading in so many books, he came to venerate Edmund Burke, who had set his face against the "antagonist world" of revolutionary destruction. One might make an interesting pamphlet of Acton's many praises of Burke, especially early in Acton's achievement: he called Burke "the teacher of mankind,"[2] and

---

[1] Gertrude Himmelfarb, *Lord Acton: A Study in Conscience and Politics* (1952; repr., Grand Rapids: Acton Institute, 2015).

[2] Acton, review of *History of the Life and Times of Edmund Burke*, by Thomas Macknight, *Rambler* n.s. (2nd ser.) 9 (April 1858): 268–73, here quoted from *SW* 1:140.

remarked that Burke's speeches from 1790 to 1795 were "the law and the prophets."[3] He agreed with Burke that the French Revolution has been "the enemy of liberty."[4]

How then did Acton come from time to time to commend revolution? Because he thought of political revolutions as bringing about, usually, an increase of freedom. Here we need to inquire what Acton meant by this freedom or liberty which was the great subject of his study, lecturing, and writing.

He meant Ciceronian and Christian concepts of liberty—ordered freedom, governed by conscience. He understood, of course, Cicero's distinction between voluntas and libido: the first is willed freedom, the freedom of the high old Roman virtue; the second is lust, the freedom of unhallowed appetites. And Acton knew, of course, the Pauline truth that "the service of God is perfect freedom." Acton understood that power is the ability to do unto other people as one wishes, whether those others so wish or not; while freedom is the ability to withstand arbitrary power. Thus true freedom is the opportunity to make moral choices, and to do one's moral duty here below. Lord Acton—who never throughout his life suffered under any arbitrary power—detested the absolutist political regimes of earlier centuries and those that remained during his own age. Part of what he meant by freedom may be gathered from the following two brief fragments extracted from his unpublished manuscripts.

> Definition of Liberty: (1) Security for minorities; (2) Reason reigning over reason, not will over will; (3) Duty to God unhindered by man; (4) Reason before will; (5) Right above might.[5]

> Liberty is the condition of duty, the guardian of conscience. It grows as conscience grows. The domains of both grow together. Liberty is safety from all hindrances, even sin. So that Liberty ends by being Free Will.[6]

---

[3] Acton to Richard Simpson, February 4, 1859, in *CLARS* 1:149, excerpted in *SW* 3:540.

[4] Add. Mss. 4955, p. 247, excerpted in *SW* 3:540.

[5] Add. Mss. 5399, p. 3, excerpted in *SW* 3:489.

[6] Add. Mss. 5006, p. 242, excerpted in *SW* 3:491.

Liberty of conscience and religious toleration were Acton's highest concerns in the pursuit of personal and civil liberty; these preoccupations made of him a Liberal Catholic, opposed to the doctrine of papal infallibility and to much else that resulted from the Vatican Council.

But we are proceeding too rapidly in describing the development of Acton's views, perhaps. In his early writings, Acton denounced revolutions as "a malady, a frenzy, an interruption of the nation's growth, sometimes fatal to its existence, often to its independence." How his views gradually changed, we may ascertain by some examination of his successive essays on political revolutions.

The earliest of these, entitled "Political Causes of the American Revolution," was published in Acton's periodical the *Rambler*, May 1861; it was not reprinted until included in Douglas Woodruff's edition of select Acton *Essays on Church and State*, in 1952. It begins with references to Athenian democracy, and continues, "The fate of every democracy, of every government based on the sovereignty of the people, depends on the choices it makes between these opposite principles, absolute power on the one hand, and on the other the restraints of legality and the authority of tradition."[7] Acton then proceeds—saying nothing whatever about the violent events of the years 1775–1786 in America—to examine the Constitution drawn up in 1787. "Far from being the product of a democratic revolution," he writes, "and of an opposition to English institutions, the constitution of the United States was the result of a powerful reaction against democracy, and in favour of the traditions of the mother country."[8]

In this remarkably percipient essay, written when Sir John Acton was twenty-seven years old and a member of Parliament, he explained the success of America's federal system of government as a guarantor of liberty, restraining national democracy, averting the domination of a temporary numerical majority. He found that Thomas Jefferson with his contempt for social and political continuity, his doctrine that

---

[7] Acton, "Political Causes of the American Revolution," *Rambler*, n.s. (3rd ser.) 5 (May 1861): 17–61, here quoted from *SW* 1:216; cf. *Essays on Church and State*, ed. Douglas Woodruff (New York: Viking, 1953), 291–338.

[8] Acton, "Political Causes of the American Revolution," in *SW* 1:219.

"the dead have no rights," his trust in the people *en masse*, "subverted the republicanism of America, and consequently the Republic itself."⁹

In a dozen printed pages, Acton discussed the general conservatism of the delegates to the Constitutional Convention, whose opinions he had studied closely. His views are very like those expressed in recent years by such American scholars as M. E. Bradford, Forrest McDonald, Daniel Boorstin, Clinton Rossiter, and your servant. Twenty-eight years later, in his lengthy review of Bryce's book *The American Commonwealth*, Acton would come to very different judgments.

All this about the Constitutional Convention of 1787? Well enough. But what about the American Revolution, an account of which is promised by the title of this major essay? Why, the revolution that Sir John Acton wrote about in this essay did not commence in 1775? No, it commenced in 1861; and nowadays we call it the American Civil War, or the War between the States.

For the secession of the Southern states, Acton argued in the following portion of his essay, was a revolution justified by resistance to the looming oppression of South by North; by the attempt of the voracious Northern industrial interest, the fanatic abolitionist, and the consolidators of national power to subject the South to an unconstitutional domination of a central government, repudiating true constitutional federalism. The tyranny of a democratic majority over a sectional minority, or of one economic interest over other economic interests, could become intolerable, and the Southerners did well to rebel against democratic despotism (as Tocqueville had called such a condition).

"It is simply the spurious democracy of the French Revolution that has destroyed the Union," Acton wrote in 1861, "by disintegrating the remnants of English traditions and institutions. All the great controversies—on the embargo, restriction, internal improvements, the Bank-Charter Act, the formation of new States, the acquisition of new territory, abolition—are phases of this mighty change, steps in the passage from a constitution framed on an English model to a system imitating that of France." "The secession of the Southern states," Acton concluded, "... is chiefly important in a political light as a protest and reaction against revolutionary doctrines, and as a

---

⁹ Acton, "Political Causes of the American Revolution," in *SW* 1:230.

move in the opposite direction to that which prevails in Europe."[10] The Confederate revolution, he judged, was a rising meant to secure liberty; the French Revolution has turned out, with its successor risings in Europe, to be the road to a hideous tyranny.

Sir John Acton, M.P., quoted with high respect and at great length John C. Calhoun on concurrent majorities; he concurred in such matters with Orestes Brownson, "the most influential journalist of America";[11] he cited Alexis de Tocqueville for authority. He exposed the injustice of protective tariffs levied by the Northern industrial interest; he assailed the abolitionists for exhibiting "the same abstract, ideal absolutism, which is equally hostile with the Catholic and with the English spirit."[12] This essay of his presents the best case for the Confederate cause made by any observer abroad, a thoroughly conservative judgment in the line of Burke and Tocqueville.

But by 1889, a radical change had occurred in Acton's judgment about the convictions and the assumptions of the delegates to the Constitutional Convention of 1787, as he had described those constitutional origins in his essay on "Political Causes of the American Revolution" in 1861. Then he had emphasized the freedom of the Framers from abstract doctrine and theoretic dogma; he had declared that the Framers were governed by respect for English institutions, custom, convention, and prescription. Yet in his criticisms of James Bryce's book *The American Commonwealth*, published in the *English Historical Review*, 1889, on finding that Bryce entertained the very judgments about the conservative attachment of the delegates of 1787 to custom, convention, and English institutions which Acton had published eighteen years early—why, Acton proceeded to contradict his eminent Liberal colleague Bryce, and to contradict himself.

For now he declared the American Revolution to have been "the supreme manifestation of the law of resistance, as the abstract revolution in its purest and most perfect shape."[13] Ignoring the judgments of Burke, Gentz, and other analysts of the American War of

---

[10] Acton, "Political Causes of the American Revolution," in *SW* 1:261–62.

[11] Acton, "Political Causes of the American Revolution," in *SW* 1:244.

[12] Acton, "Political Causes of the American Revolution," in *SW* 1:258.

[13] Acton, review of *The American Commonwealth*, by James Bryce, *English Historical Review* 4 (1889): 388–96, here quoted from *SW* 1:404.

Independence, Acton now insisted that the Americans fought not for constitutional rights, what Burke had called "the chartered rights of Englishmen," but for abstract liberty. Why should they have counted the cost, and why should we? For the American Revolution taught that

> men ought to be in arms even against a remote and constructive danger to their freedom; that even if the cloud is no bigger than a man's hand, it is their right and duty to stake the national existence, to sacrifice lives and fortunes, to cover the country with a lake of blood, to shatter crowns and scepters and fling parliaments into the sea. On this principle of subversion they erected their commonwealth, and by its virtue lifted the world out of its orbit and assigned a new course to history. Here or nowhere we have the broken chain, the rejected past, precedent and statute superseded by unwritten law, sons wiser than their fathers, ideas rooted in the future, reason cutting as clean as Atropos.[14]

Fine rhetoric. But this exhortation to "sound, sound the clarion, fill the fife," and for other men to wade through lakes of blood in advancement of abstract principle, seems a trifle false, coming from the country house of a middle-aged nobleman who never struck a blow, dwelling in the security of Victorian England or Hohenzollern Germany. Acton had read Marx, and had urged his great friend Gladstone to do so. In this rhetoric about the American Revolution, do we hear an echo of Marx's doctrine of massive bloodletting to achieve the final revolution?

Some of us are wiser in our youth than in our middle years; so it seems to have been with Acton. Perhaps there had been growing in Acton's imagination an infatuation with revolution—and not merely with revolution in the realm of ideas. For it was his assumption, which seems naïve to us nowadays, that all revolutions against established and complacent authority would lead, at least in the long run, toward greater genuine freedom for everyman.

That postulate runs through Acton's lectures on modern history, delivered at Cambridge at the turn of the century. He approved the bloodshed of the Puritan Revolution—that is, the English Civil

---

[14] Acton, review of *The American Commonwealth*, in *SW* 1:404.

Wars—because it brought down Stuart absolutism, even if it raised up Cromwell; he approved the English Revolution (of 1688), even though it dethroned a Catholic king and began struggles that lasted until 1745. For despite faults, the Act of Settlement, Acton said, "is the greatest thing done by the English nation," establishing parliamentary supremacy in administration as well as in legislation.[15] Acton's lecture approving the American Revolution (this time, really about the fighting that began in 1775) is more temperate, consistent with Burke's speeches from 1765 to 1775. Acton points out, however, that the British in North America had suffered no oppression; "There was no tyranny to be resented. The colonists were in many ways more completely their own masters than Englishmen at home."[16] But he seems to glory in Lexington, Concord, and Bunker Hill.

This acceptance or even enthusiastic approbation of revolutionary violence did not well consist with Acton's subscription to the principle that the means are not justified by the end, or with his condemnation of murder as the worst of sins. Ralph Waldo Emerson (despised by Acton) instructs us that "a foolish consistency is the hobgoblin of little minds"; elsewhere I have commented that a fatuous optimism frequently is the damnation of expansive minds. Acton, over and over again, expressed his confidence that the universal growth of conscience would end in perfect, or nearly perfect, universal liberty. This is to ignore the Christian dogma of original sin. In the interest of making progress on the road to that Zion of conscience, Acton was prepared to excuse considerable slaughter.

Consider his uneasy judgment of the judicial murder of Charles I, Archbishop Laud, and Lord Strafford by Cromwell's regicide Parliament. "We cannot avoid the question," Acton wrote,

> whether the three great victims ... deserved their fate. It is certain that they were put to death illegally, and therefore unjustly.... But we have no thread through the enormous intricacy and complexity of modern politics except the idea of progress towards more perfect and assured freedom, and the divine right of free men. Judged by that test, the three cul-

---

[15] Acton, *LMH*, 231; *SW* 1:119.

[16] Acton, *LMH*, 309; *SW* 1:192.

prits must be condemned. That is a principle which cuts very
deep, and reaches far, and we must be prepared to see how
it applies in thousands of other instances, in other countries,
and in other times, especially the times in which we live.[17]

Do we not find in Acton's preceding sentence the implication that
men and women so foolish as to stand in the way, wittingly or unwit-
tingly, of some grand principle—of liberty, say—must be thrust aside,
or "liquidated," as the ideologues of the twentieth century would put
it? There comes to mind Madame Roland's lamentation, "O Liberty,
what crimes are committed in thy name!" At the time of his lecture
on the Puritan Revolution, Acton was deep in preparation for his
succeeding lectures on the French Revolution. Were Louis XVI,
Marie Antoinette, and thousands of others in other countries, among
culprits providentially condemned? Aye, and even Madame Roland,
too? King Charles, Strafford, and Laud had been no enthusiasts for
a vague universal liberty, attained through perfection of conscience;
therefore their heads had to be taken off, if illegally and unjustly—a
noble paradox.

Near the end of his life, Lord Acton seemingly had come to relish
abstract doctrine and theoretic dogma, which he abjured in his essay
"Political Causes of the American Revolution" nearly two decades
earlier. Had the slogan "Liberty, Equality, Fraternity" waked something inconsistent and injudicious in him, abhorrent to him though
the consequences—the immediate terrors—of the French Revolution
were? In his lecture on the Puritan Revolution, is there some suggestion of Marx's inexorable divinized or personified History, along
whose juggernaut path reactionaries must be crushed to earth? Acton
thought that in history he discerned the march of Providence. Yet it
may be perilous to confound Providence with History. And may not
Providence be retributory, as well as beneficent?

In his inaugural lecture as Regius Professor of Modern History at
Cambridge (1895), Acton contended that History reveals the march
of Providence toward greater freedom. He hoped that "history will aid
you to see that the action of Christ who is risen on mankind whom
he redeemeth fails not, but increases; that the wisdom of divine rule

---

[17] Acton, *LMH*, 202–3; *SW* 1:95.

appears not in the perfection but in the improvement of the world; and that achieved liberty is the one ethical result that rests on the converging and combined conditions of advancing civilisation. Then you will understand what a famous philosopher said, that History is the true demonstration of Religion." (Here Acton refers to Leibniz.)[18]

But later in this same famous inaugural lecture, the Regius Professor experienced misgivings. Is it not violent revolution, rather than historical reflection and the increasing reign of conscience, that causes great changes for the better in mankind's liberty? Was not he contradicting himself?

"If the supreme conquests of society are won more often by violence than by lenient arts," Lord Acton told his auditors,

> if the trend and drift of things is towards convulsions and catastrophes, if the world owes religious liberty to the Dutch Revolution, constitutional government to the English, federal republicanism to the American, political equality to the French and its successors, what is to become of us, docile and attentive students of the absorbing Past? The triumph of the Revolutionist annuls the historian. By its authentic exponents, Jefferson and Sieyès, the Revolution of the last century repudiates history. Their followers renounced acquaintance with it, and were ready to destroy its records and to abolish its inoffensive professors.[19]

Might Acton himself, after a fashion, be renouncing history in these late years of his? He had begun to distance himself from Burke. For Burke was the champion of custom, convention, prescription, precedent; and therefore dwelt in the dead past; while he, Acton, thrusting aside custom and convention, flinging off that dead hand of the past, was the champion of present and future, guiding himself not by past experience of mankind, but by truthful principle, which would work wonders. He had begun to sound like Thomas Jefferson, muttering "The dead have no rights."

Answering his own question concerning what might become of "docile and attentive students of the absorbing Past," Acton observed,

---

[18] Acton, *LMH*, 12; *SW* 3:521–23.

[19] Acton, *LMH*, 13–14; *SW* 3:525–26.

somewhat lamely, that revolutionary events, however violent, had worked some healthy reaction in the minds of the more intelligent, stimulating afresh their interest in history. Conservative and Liberal schools of historical interpretation had sprung up during the nineteenth century. Vastly important archives had been opened to the scholarly historian. As a result, it had become possible to make nearer approaches to historical truth. Conscience was at work—tutored conscience, not merely the confused conscience of private judgment. Be of good cheer as the nineteenth century draws to its close. Is not Liberalism in the ascendant?

At last we come to Lord Acton's *Lectures on the French Revolution*, delivered for the fourth time at Cambridge University three years before his death, and published in 1910. The book is lucid and accurate, reflecting Acton's thoroughness of method and immense reading and investigation of documents; it remains worthy to stand alongside the volumes on the French Revolution by Tocqueville, Taine, and Carlyle; it may be supplemented by Schama's impressive *Citizens: A Chronicle of the French Revolution* (1989). Acton knew that some revolution in French affairs was needed; but the revolution which arrived was the pulverizing of freedom. It seemed in its violence to refute Acton's premise that successive revolutions would forever put an end to the arbitrary state.

"By a series of violent shocks the nations in succession have struggled to shake off the Past, to reverse the action of Time and the verdict of success, and to rescue the world from the reign of the dead," Acton had said in his lecture on the beginning of the modern state, in his series on modern history.[20] Had indeed the French Revolution been a work of rescue? Somehow things had gone wrong from the first, in 1789, and Acton recognized that unpleasant truth. The Declaration of the Rights of Man was founded upon fallacies, Acton perceived. Amazingly, Gertrude Himmelfarb, in her biography of Acton, endeavors to persuade her readers that "Acton had nothing but praise" for that Declaration of the Rights of Man and

---

[20] Acton, *LMH*, 32; *SW* 3:639.

the Citizen.[21] Are we to regard as *praise* the following passage from his seventh lecture on the Revolution?

> The Declaration passed, by August 26, after a hurried debate, and with no further resistance. The Assembly, which had abolished the past at the beginning of the month, attempted, at the end, to institute and regulate the future. These are its abiding works, and the perpetual heritage of the Revolution. With them a new era dawned upon mankind.
>
> And yet this single page of print, which outweighs libraries, and is stronger than all the armies of Napoleon, is not the work of superior minds, and bears no mark of the lion's claw. The stamp of Cartesian clearness is upon it, but without the logic, the precision, the thoroughness of French thought. There is no indication in it that Liberty is the goal, and not the starting-point, that it is a faculty to be acquired, not a capital to invest, or that it depends on the union of innumerable conditions, which embrace the entire life of man. Therefore it is justly arraigned by those who say that it is defective, and that its defects have been a peril and a snare.[22]

From this Declaration of the Rights of Man and the Citizen, the road of the French led with swiftly increasing violence to catastrophe, the revolution soon devouring its own children—a terrible story Acton relates unsparingly. The passion for liberty trampled out order and justice; and tolerable societies require the reality of all three principles.

The Jacobin cry for liberty devastated the European continent, and was prevented from working the ruin of civilization only by force and a master. "I have laid the fell spirit of Innovation that was striding over all the world," Napoleon Bonaparte boasted.

Of course this Jacobin notion of liberty was not what Acton desired; nor did he applaud at all the notion of equality, and the only fraternity he acknowledged was *Christian* brotherhood. The liberty of his imagination was very much a British liberty, developed over seven centuries by much continuity of belief and institution, with merely an occasional revolution—of limited scope—to accelerate progress some-

---

[21] Himmelfarb, *Lord Acton: A Study in Conscience and Politics*, 194.

[22] Acton, *LFR*, 107.

what. He and his friend Gladstone shared the Victorian expectation of universal progress; they might even be called meliorists, were it not for that doctrine of revolution as a goad.

A dozen years after Lord Acton's death in 1902, the world entered upon what Arnold Toynbee called a time of troubles—a time which, if we may believe another distinguished historian, Fernand Braudel, may end with the arrival of the twenty-first century. The cry "liberty!" has been heard in nearly every country since 1914; but what has been attained in most of the world is tyranny. Revolution of the most violent character has reduced most of Africa and Asia to misery; eastern Europe only now begins to hope for some restoration of order. Latin America, or much of it, remains in convulsions. The expectation of Acton that revolution would be an instrument of progress and emancipation has been exploded. On the contrary, in the twentieth century the word revolution has come to signify, commonly, an occasion for the proletariat to loot the quarters of the prosperous—and perhaps to slit throats, too. As Burke declared, at the end of every revolutionary vista stands the guillotine.

I commend to you an essay, entitled "This Terrible Century," by Gerhart Niemeyer, in the Fall 1993 number of *The Intercollegiate Review*. "To us, who are enjoying a life in relative wealth, the educational and artistic offerings of a flourishing culture, and, yes, in peace, this century may appear to provide full reason for self-congratulation," Niemeyer writes. "To the future historian, however, it may rank as one of the worst centuries of human history. That is, it may so appear to an historian who can discern between good and evil spirits, who is sensitive to the needs of the soul and skillful in reading between the lines of official texts.... He may wonder at the phenomenon of totalitarianism ... a novelty in history, and at government by ideology that produced *general slavery*, while formerly only private slavery had occurred."[23]

Lord Acton was eminent among those historians who distinguish between good and evil spirits, are sensitive to the needs of the soul, and are skillful in interpreting archives. With what horror Acton would look upon the closing decade of our twentieth century! The

---

[23] Gerhart Niemeyer, "This Terrible Century," *Intercollegiate Review* 29, no. 1 (Fall 1993): 3 (emphasis in original).

demand for greater liberty still is heard upon every hand, but the demand in this country is for "lifestyle liberty," the freedom of the libido, not the freedom of *voluntas*. The inhabitants of Bosnia are set free to slaughter one another. An alleged freedom is being conferred just now upon the Bantu in South Africa that may repeat the horror of the emancipated Congo three decades past. In what country do we encounter that happy increase of the influence of conscience which Acton preaches?

Freedom cannot endure except upon the footing of a healthy order—order in the soul, and order in the commonwealth. Revolution, after all, is the disruption of order, and therefore extreme medicine. For that reason, the serious student of history today will do well to rank such historians as Eric Voegelin and Christopher Dawson—historians of order—higher than Acton. Nevertheless, I take great pleasure in reading Acton's essays on liberty repeatedly, and do commend them to you. Lord Acton, now a member of the community of souls, you and all the dead do have rights, Jefferson notwithstanding; for, my lord, you are one of those souls now in eternity who give energy to us the living; and I pray that you may continue to be read in a revolutionary age oppressed by Giant Ideology.

8

THE LEGACY OF AN EDUCATION*

James C. Holland

How are we to understand the continuing interest in Lord Acton?
He was, after all, remote from popular culture in his time: he
was an aristocrat (the only child of the Duchess of Dalberg), an intellectual, a professor, and a Catholic whose thought often disquieted
church authority. Except to the rare observer of his occasional flash
of brilliance in a social setting, he was not prominent in the popular
mind. No, it is not owing to his public record that Acton lives on in
our memories; rather, it is for his ideas that his name continues to
be honored. Yearly, the name Acton appears hundreds of times in
books, pamphlets, articles, and in learned and not-so-learned talks.
The telling truth is that we must look to his highly exceptional education for the answer to the question, for it was his education that left
him with a remarkable set of beliefs, at once fascinating and provok-
ing to posterity.

There were a good half-dozen distinct and formative influences in
John Acton's schooling: (1) an easy familiarity with the leadership and
functioning of the ecclesiastical world; (2) a passion for history, books,
and manuscripts; (3) behind-the-scenes exposure to revolutionary

---

*Originally given as the Lord Acton Lecture at the Acton Institute,
January 1997.

changes in the historian's craft then underway in German universities; (4) personal entrée to vast, newly opening archival collections on the Continent; (5) training in a philosophy of history that led to his lifelong preoccupation with the history of freedom; and finally, (6) the fostering of a devout, nondogmatic Christian faith. My purpose here is to argue that these elements in Acton's intellectual formation shaped the expanse of his intellect which, in turn, established his place in history.

The earliest distinctive feature in Acton's education, something that remained a constant throughout his formative years, was an easy familiarity with the clerical world. His uncle was a bishop, then a cardinal. In 1842, at the age of eight, he spent a few months as a student at Saint Nicholas de Chardonnet, near Paris, under the direction of Felix Dupanloup, later bishop. The next five years (1842–1847) were spent at Saint Mary's College, Oscott, near Birmingham, under Nicholas Wiseman, then bishop and soon to become the first Cardinal Archbishop of Westminster. Finally, after two years of study in Scotland (under still other clergymen), he went to Munich at the age of sixteen for nearly five years of university studies guided by the celebrated priest-historian, Ignaz von Döllinger. Acton was never intimidated or otherwise inhibited by cassocks, miters, red hats, or even the tiara.

It was while at Oscott that Acton discovered his passion for history. Wiseman had made the place an intellectual clearinghouse for English Catholics, especially clergy—particularly converts from the Oxford Movement. Years later Acton reflected on Wiseman and the atmosphere of the place: "We used to see him with Lord Shrewsbury, with O'Connell, with Pugin, and we had a feeling that Oscott, next to Pekin, was a centre of the world."[1]

From Oscott this eight-year-old child wrote exuberant letters to his mother: "I am going to write a sort of compendium of the chief facts, in history, for my own occasional reference."[2] He had signed

---

[1] Acton, quoted in Wilfrid Ward, *The Life and Times of Cardinal Wiseman*, 2 vols. (London: Longmans, Green, and Co., 1897), 1:348–49.

[2] Acton to Lady Leveson, n.d., in *Correspondence*, 2.

an earlier letter, "Caesar, Agamemnon, John Dahlberg Acton."[3] Soon he was complaining that he needed a private room. "When I get a room I shall study History very much. I intend to get several books about it."[4] At once he commenced writing of a related passion: "As I mean to have a perfect library in my room, I should be much obliged to you to bring me from Paris some books of French literature. I should particularly like a good edition of the Histoire des Croisades, and the History of France. As to the present you promised me, I should very much like the Biographical Dictionary."[5] His letters became a veritable litany of appreciation for volumes received as gifts, spanning in subject the classical world, Saint Thomas More, and contemporary France. These modest gatherings at Oscott would become the nucleus of his vast and magnificent seventy-thousand volume personal library, now held as a special collection of the Cambridge University Library.

After five years of rigorous studies in the classics, languages, literature, history, and religion, Johnny Acton was eager to move on from a place where he said that "memories are taxed too much." Also, Acton's stepfather, Lord Granville, an eminent Whig who had succeeded to the peerage in 1846, was not pleased with the limitations at Oscott.[6] He believed that the boy needed improvement in Latin, Greek, English, mathematics, and history before applying to one of the Cambridge colleges where Acton's father and uncle had gone.

---

[3] Acton to Lady Leveson, February 15, 1844, in *Correspondence*, 2.

[4] Acton to Lady Leveson, n.d., quoted in James C. Holland, "The Education of Lord Acton" (PhD diss., Catholic University of America, 1968), 26.

[5] Acton to Lady Leveson, n.d., quoted in Holland, "The Education of Lord Acton," 26.

[6] Granville thought that he was educating a future political leader for the Whig establishment and was concerned that Acton's education prepare him accordingly. He pushed the move to Edinburgh, which became one more complication in their lifelong strained relationship. In his biography, Roland Hill argues persuasively that Acton's recurring bouts with loneliness stemmed from his mother's second marriage, a union that Hill believes stripped Acton of the emotional nourishment that he craved and rarely received.

Granville arranged for two years of private tutoring in Edinburgh in the home and under the direction of Henry John Charles Logan, a cleric and former vice president of Oscott. Johnny Acton called these years his "polar exile" passed "in a town that was built for study," the cold wind and short days offering few distractions from fireside, conversation, and books.

Herbert Butterfield observed that Acton left Scotland "a regular schoolboy Whig ... brimming with cocksureness, and primed with 'Macaulayism.'"[7] In fact two volumes of Macaulay's five-volume *History of England* had been published by that time, and by his own admission Acton read them four times![8] Doubtless this beginning of his political education—he discovered Burke there as well—pleased his Whig stepfather. Forget for a moment the flaws of the Whig theory of history; remember only its overarching story of liberty triumphing over tyranny in seventeenth-century England, of representative aristocratic institutions thwarting the best efforts of the Stuart kings to concentrate power. The sheer drama of this tale excited Johnny Acton's precocious mind and remained with him long after he discarded the exaggerations of Whiggery.

At the very time Acton applied for admission to three Cambridge colleges—the fall of 1850—there was a national upheaval over the formal restoration of the Roman Catholic hierarchy to England, which had been suppressed since the Reformation. His rejection by all three colleges was, in fact, not personal but the consequence of a surge in cultural anti-Catholicism. In retrospect, his rejection proved to be the greatest blessing of his life. Forced to look elsewhere for her son, Lady Granville contacted her relations in Munich, the Count and Countess Arco-Valley, who were close friends of the accomplished scholar, Ignaz von Döllinger. At once, Döllinger agreed to direct Acton's university studies, and for the next four years the student was all but inseparable from "the Professor," as the great teacher would be known ever after.

---

[7] Herbert Butterfield, "Acton: His Training, Methods and Intellectual System," in *Studies in Diplomatic History and Historiography*, ed. A. O. Sarkissian (London: Longmans, 1961), 170.

[8] Acton to Lady Granville, May 21, [1848], Add. Mss. 8121(7)/494.

These were the happiest years of Acton's life, these years of study and travel, when exciting things were happening in German universities and Continental libraries and archives. Through the influence of his two major professors—Döllinger and Peter Ernst von Lasaulx—Acton formed the core of the intellectual perspective that guided his efforts for the remainder of his years.

It was at Munich that he found emotional peace, so desperately desired, in the warmth of the Arco-Valley household, in their city residence, in their castle near Ried in Upper Austria, and in their country villa on Tegernsee, where Döllinger himself was a frequent guest. Acton fashioned an immediate, intense, and affectionate attachment to the Countess, whom he visited often and with whom he took long carriage rides in the country. She became a second mother, listening to his every care, filling a void occasioned by his natural mother's marriage to Lord Granville. Lady Granville's heavy duties as one of the principal hostesses during the English social and political seasons left inadequate time for her son. Fifteen years later Johnny Acton married his cousin, the Countess's daughter, Marie.

Döllinger was himself the intellectual heir to an expansive Catholic scholarship in historical studies dating from the revolutionary reforms that Bonaparte imposed on the Germanies. After the 1803 Act of Secularization, there were no exclusively Catholic or Protestant states in the Holy Roman Empire. As a result, Catholic and Protestant scholars were thrust into one another's societies, for the first time having to labor side by side in universities, libraries, and archives. To the Protestant university at Tübingen in 1817 came the Catholic faculty in theology from Ellwangen. This was a development of momentous significance to Catholic intellectual life in the Germanies.

The ground began to shift in Catholic theological circles. Through the work of a few eminent theologians, including Johann Sebastian von Drey (1777–1853) and Johann Adam Möhler (1796–1838), German Catholic thought embraced the concept of history-sensitive doctrinal development. The touchstone of Drey's plea was continuity of belief within a framework of developing theological definition, while Möhler nurtured the idea of the church as Christ living in history. That concept was the chief attainment of the Tübingen school. Möhler moved to the Munich faculty in 1835 through the efforts of Döllinger and was instrumental in turning Döllinger to historical studies as they pertained to theology. This was a fateful move. As Stephen Tonsor has written, "it was history which led him to the idea of the development of Christian doctrine and eventually into a position branded by his opponents as heretical."[9]

Döllinger was soon a prime advocate of the new school of historical theology, holding that the historical record, objectively examined and understood, would reveal the deceits and misconceptions of the ages as well as explain the "unfolding" of the doctrines of the Christian faith from earliest times. He believed that a knowledge of the interaction of history and theology afforded the surest means for dislodging time-honored errors and vindicating the essential claims of historic Catholicism. Döllinger never doubted the providential nature of history. Indeed, to his mind, the appearance of error in history, even evil itself, served but to stimulate further "unfolding" of doctrinal truth as a corrective. Acton recalled the intellectual atmosphere:

> As an historian, Döllinger regarded Christianity as a force more than as a doctrine, and displayed it as it expanded and became the soul of later history. It was the mission and occupation of his life to discover and to disclose how this was accomplished, and to understand the history of civilised Europe, religious and profane, mental and political, by the aid of sources which, being original and authentic, yielded certainty.[10]

Acton attended Döllinger's lectures on early church history, the Middle Ages, the church since the French Revolution, and the philosophy of religion. Significantly, the Professor also insisted that Acton study theology for three full years.

When Acton arrived in Munich, the Professor was writing his church history, but his earlier three volumes on the Reformation (1846–1848) and his biography of Luther (1850) already reflected the new spirit. Though he lamented Protestantism's break with continu-

---

[9] Stephen J. Tonsor, "Lord Acton on Döllinger's Historical Theology," *Journal of the History of Ideas* 20, no. 3 (June–September 1959): 331.

[10] Acton, "Döllinger's Historical Work," *English Historical Review* 5 (1890): 700–744, here quoted from *SW* 2:419.

ity and development, Döllinger portrayed Luther in heroic terms as a German national figure, something unheard of in earlier Catholic scholarship. It must be remembered that both Döllinger and Acton were convinced that the new scholarship would sustain the claims of Catholicism in the end. But they also believed that painful admission of historic wrongdoing by church authorities at the highest level must first be acknowledged. However exciting the promise of the new learning, however esteemed its proponents, anxieties were aroused in powerful quarters. Church leaders feared that revelations of specific wrongdoing might well beget widespread scandal and confusion among the faithful masses. And the new learning itself, with its demand for free intellectual inquiry, was perceived as a threat to the very foundation of episcopal authority. Moreover, the atmosphere was exacerbated by the rise of a strident and intensely anticlerical Italian nationalism that threatened the continued existence of the eleven-centuries-old Papal States. Understandably, many ecclesiastical leaders viewed the new learning as but one more threat in a rapidly secularizing world.

Second only to Döllinger in influence among Acton's Munich professors was Peter Ernst von Lasaulx, under whom Acton studied Greek history and literature, aesthetics, art history, and the philosophy of history. For it was Lasaulx who introduced Acton to the history of ideas. Lasaulx viewed all history as an unbroken tale, a continuous flow, and he believed that religion drove the core impulse for human advancement through the rise and fall of civilizations. He put it this way: "All history is in the last analysis a history of religion; thus Christianity as the universal religion of the world has absorbed all prior national religions in so far as they contained truth. There is hardly one truth expressed in Christianity that according to its substance could not be found in the pre-Christian era."[11]

Again we see the focus on history and historical process as the key to understanding both religious development and the claims of authority in religion. Fearful of the implications of his work, Rome consigned nearly all of Lasaulx's philosophical writings to the Index of Prohibited Books, notably his 1856 *Philosophie der Geschichte*, of which Acton later wrote, "since Schlegel, so brilliant a work has not

---

[11] Quoted in Friedrich Engel-Janosi, "The Historical Thought of Ernst von Lasaulx," *Theological Studies* 14, no. 3 (September 1953): 385.

145

appeared on the same field."[12] When Lasaulx died in 1861, Acton purchased nearly the entirety of his extensive library, especially prizing the many books annotated by his old professor.

A third historian who influenced significantly Acton's training in history was Leopold von Ranke, who was in the vanguard of those scholars who benefited from the opening of archival collections. He believed that access to archives and stern scientific methodology made it possible to evoke the past with precision and certitude. Though unsuccessful, Döllinger had actually tried to bring Ranke to Munich from the University of Berlin. Yet it was Döllinger who developed ambivalent thoughts regarding the "scientific school," seeing the threat of secularization in a Trojan horse. Acton, on the other hand, who came under Ranke's influence near the close of his Munich education, embraced the "scientific" regimen with the zeal of a convert.[13]

Such was the distinctive zeitgeist of Acton's education, and he immersed himself into this world fully and with stupendous energy. He appreciated that there was nothing comparable outside the German-speaking world. Moreover, for nearly three years following 1854, though no longer under formal instruction, Acton spent long periods with the Professor both in Munich and in travel, visiting archives and scholars of renown, deepening his knowledge, and expanding his enthusiasm for the new learning.

Let us now turn to the question, How did Acton's education shape his mature thought? What imprint did it have on the labors of his life? For the purpose at hand, I will consider four illustrations: (1) his achievements in journalism, (2) his dealings with church authority, (3) his friendship with William Ewart Gladstone, and (4) his conclusion that the historian, in writing history, must exercise moral judgment in redressing the crimes of history.

Acton began his career in journalism as soon as he returned to England early in 1858. Filled with the treasure of the new learning,

---

[12] Acton, "Mr. Buckle's Philosophy of History," *Rambler*, n.s. (2nd ser.) 10 (August 1858): 88–104, here quoted from *SW* 3:449.

[13] Butterfield, "Acton: His Training, Methods and Intellectual System," 188.

he was eager to return home to raise the intellectual level of his coreligionists. For this purpose he acquired controlling interest in a modest Catholic journal, the *Rambler*, explaining to the Professor: "It will give me a position and an influence among Catholics which I hope to use well ... I reflected also that it was an opportunity of doing great good which I was most fortunate to obtain that from my knowledge of persons abroad ... that it was a capital means of turning my German studies to account."[14]

From February 1858, until April 1864, Acton was engaged as owner, manager, and writer for two successive journals, the *Rambler* until May 1862, then the *Home and Foreign Review* until April 1864. Joined by others, including John Henry Newman, he and his literary partner, Richard Simpson, a convert from the Anglican priesthood, who, unlike Acton, was blessed with a marvelous sense of humor, set about probing and prodding a host of subjects ranging from education and literature to history and theology. At the same time they insisted on free intellectual inquiry as the surest path for reaching truth, whatever the topic.

Troubles soon arose from two quarters. In an age of narrow sectarian animosities, ecclesiastical authority did not take kindly to open positions openly arrived at, especially by laymen; the *Rambler* circle soon found itself *persona non grata* in Catholic power centers stretching from London to Rome. Even more disheartening was the response of the great mass of the laity, who did not seem even to grasp the message, and in a dark hour of a particular controversy Acton counseled Simpson: "It seems absurd for me to take the prudent line, considering my insufficiently disguised contempt for every unscientific method of treating literary and political and ecclesiastical matters, but I have learnt by experience the uselessness of addressing people in a tone they do not understand, and supposing knowledge which does not exist."[15]

After six years crowded with conflict, misunderstanding, and mounting tension between the journals and church authority, and

---

[14] Acton to Döllinger, February 17, 1858, in Johann Joseph Ignaz von Döllinger, *Briefwechsel 1820–1890*, ed. Victor Conzemius, 3 vols. (Munich: Beck, 1963–1971), 1:128.

[15] Acton to Döllinger, February 17, 1858, in Döllinger, *Briefwechsel*, 1:128.

facing imminent censure by that authority, Acton decided to abandon the effort. Both heart and mind were revealed in bidding his readers farewell: "It was but a partial and temporary embodiment of an imperishable idea—the faint reflection of a light which still lives and burns in the hearts of the silent thinkers of the Church."[16]

It remained for the astute Protestant skeptic, Matthew Arnold, to note the profound accomplishment of the Acton circle when he wrote of the *Home and Foreign Review*, "perhaps in no organ of criticism in this country was there so much knowledge, so much play of mind."[17] The genesis of that knowledge and "play of mind," its precise tone and substance, can be traced to Munich.

Both the *Rambler* and the *Home and Foreign Review* were frequently at odds with the preferences of ecclesiastical authority on issues relating to education, history, theology, and the principle of free intellectual inquiry. But far and away the most substantive illustration of Acton's dealing with church authority centered on his prominent role in the Vatican Council of 1869–1870, best remembered for its definition of the doctrine of papal infallibility. Acton—and Döllinger with him—were much opposed to the proposed doctrine on historical grounds that have yet to be refuted. Through scholarship and personal influence, they worked mightily to prevent its being approved by the bishops. Armed with vast learning and access to those in high places, both academic and political, the two men brought their full weight to bear on behalf of the bishops who opposed the doctrine.

Acton, just raised to the peerage through the efforts of his friend Gladstone, went to Rome to assist the efforts of the 140 prelates of the Minority, as they were called. This is an extraordinary story that is little known today. A young layman of thirty-five organized the bishops, provided them with historical arguments against the definition, boosted their morale and courage time and again, and even on occasion admonished them to hold firm in the face of intense pressure to relent. All the while he conducted an aggressive correspondence

---

[16] Acton, "Conflicts with Rome," *Home and Foreign Review* 4 (April 1864): 667–96, here quoted from *SW* 3:259.

[17] Matthew Arnold, "The Function of Criticism at the Present Time," *Essays in Criticism* (London: Macmillan, 1928), 20, quoted in Josef L. Altholz, *The Liberal Catholic Movement in England* (London: Burns & Oates, 1962), 206.

with high political authorities in Austria, France, Italy, Prussia, and above all, England, in an effort to bring governmental intervention to prevent promulgation. But it all came to naught as nearly the entirety of the opposition crumbled by the end of the Council, and the governments failed to act. Though he was more fortunate than the Professor, who was eventually excommunicated, it was a crushing blow for Acton, revealing to him the futility of his earlier hopes for bringing intellectual reform to the church. But that is another story that lies beyond our purpose here.

Writing to Lord Clarendon, the British foreign secretary, Odo Russell, Britain's observer at Rome, had this to say about Lord Acton's role at the Vatican Council:

> The strong ties that now unite the leading theological minds of England, France, Germany, Hungary and Austria are due to Lord Acton's personal influence, profound knowledge, great talents and high virtues. Without his personal intervention the bishops of the opposition could scarcely have known each other. Without his knowledge of language and of theology the theologians of the various nations represented in the Council could not have understood each other, without his talents as a leader they could not have remained united amongst each other and without his high virtues they could not have accepted and followed the lead of a layman so much younger than any of the Fathers of the Council.[18]

Had Russell known Acton better, he might well have added that it was, in fact, Acton's Germanic learning that made possible his role at the Council.

The Acton-Gladstone relationship began in 1861 when Gladstone read Acton's article on the causes of the great American Civil War. Gladstone was moved by what he read, expressing his appreciation in a letter to Acton, who was Gladstone's junior by a quarter century. What followed, for thirty-seven years, was one of the great intellectual

---

[18] Russell to the Earl of Clarendon, June 18, 1870, in Odo Russell, *The Roman Question: Extracts from the Despatches of Odo Russell from Rome, 1858–1870*, ed. Noel Blakiston (London: Chapman & Hall, 1962), 446.

companionships of the Victorian era. Gladstone, that most deliberate and durable of politicians, and Acton, the supreme student of the history of ideas, met on the common ground of insatiable curiosity.

Acton was now the mentor, receiving endless queries from the most powerful man in British public life. Their dialogue roamed the universes of antiquity, literature, history, philosophy, politics, theology, and more. From time to time Acton would despatch boxes of books from his enormous library or provide exhaustive lists of authorities to be consulted. Indeed, on occasion Gladstone had to beg off his heavy assignments so as to have time to conduct the affairs of Her Majesty's government. But he never tired of expressing his great gratitude for receiving the benefits of Acton's awesome and seemingly inexhaustible learning. Owen Chadwick sums up their relationship in this way: "They discussed everything. To Gladstone he was a sage with the highest of ethical ideals, in religion, politics or private life." Then, quoting Acton's favorite child, Mamy, Chadwick goes on to say: "Gladstone once told Acton to his face that he trusted him 'more entirely than any other man.'"[19]

Of all the interests they shared and discussed, none approached in magnitude the interplay between religion and politics, which is precisely where Acton would focus his powers.

Evaluation of Acton's commitment to moral judgment in history is more complex. Ever since his student days at Oscott, nothing so attracted his energies as the study of history. It became for him the essential path to understanding humankind in all of its triumph and tragedy. At Munich he discovered that history was a science in methodology that if properly pursued could reveal the hidden truths of the ages, secular and divine. Little by little he came to appreciate that the universal threat to unfolding truth in history was the corrupting propensity of power, all power, to skew its errors and conceal its crimes. To Gladstone's daughter Mary, he wrote in 1881: "Being refused at Cambridge, and driven to foreign universities, I never had any contemporaries, but spent years in looking for men wise enough

---

[19] Owen Chadwick, *Acton and Gladstone*, The Creighton Lecture in History 1975 (London: Athlone, 1976), 29; Acton to Mamy, May 23, 1898, Add. Mss., box 22.

to solve the problems that puzzled me, not in religion or politics so much as along the wavy line between the two."[20]

It was along that "wavy line" between religion and politics that Acton discerned the history of freedom unfolding down through recorded time. He understood with utter clarity that freedom—that "delicate fruit of a mature civilization"—cannot exist without the restraint of power, both in church and state. For him, the ultimate requisite for the existence of freedom was the sanctity of individual conscience.

The concept of an emerging "reign of conscience" became the centerpiece of Acton's commitment to moral judgment in history. From his Munich professors and others he learned that there is meaning and certitude in history. His own Christian faith, powerfully shaped by his Munich years, was deep, devout, and informed by history; it sustained him through the many public and private crises of his life. Döllinger had shown that Christianity is a body of thought in time and place, embodied in an institutional church whose teachings and authority have been shaped by historical forces. Thus, the progression of Acton's thought was as inevitable as it was relentless: Revelation has removed ambiguity from the moral arena; crime can no longer take refuge in ignorance; it therefore follows that all criminal behavior must be summoned before the magistrate of impartial history. Only thus can the tireless, corrupting propensity of power be held in check and the reign of conscience be secured.

Acton concluded that no individual or institution is exempt from the historian's dispassionate scrutiny, that no office holder is sanctified by the office held, and that no concealment of wrongdoing, however sacred the cause being served, is to be spared exposure and censure. Though long recognizing that he was isolated in his essential position, Acton never compromised the message. He put it forcefully in his inaugural lecture as Regius Professor of Modern History at Cambridge in June 1895:

> The historians of former ages, unapproachable for us in knowledge and in talent, cannot be our limit. We have the

---

[20] Acton to Mary Gladstone, June 3, 1881, in *Letters of Lord Acton to Mary, Daughter of the Right Hon. W. E. Gladstone*, ed. Herbert Paul (London: G. Allen, 1904), 104.

power to be more rigidly impersonal, disinterested and just than they; and to learn from undisguised and genuine records to look with remorse upon the past, and to the future with assured hope of better things; bearing this in mind, that if we lower our standard in history, we cannot uphold it in Church or State.[21]

Yet the most eloquent utterance of his position was given in November of that year, when he addressed, in the privacy of his rooms in Trinity's Nevile's Court, the Cambridge Eranus, a select society numbering not more than twelve. Professor Lord Acton recalled his prodigious labors years earlier in libraries and archives, and he spoke of justice and hope and the writing of history:

> There is no other way to compel assent, or to crush interest and prejudice.
>
> To renounce the pains and penalties of exhaustive research is to remain a victim to ill informed and designing writers, and to authorities that have worked for ages to build up the vast tradition of conventional mendacity.
>
> By going on from book to manuscript and from library to archive, we exchange doubt for certainty, and become our own masters. We explore a new heaven and a new earth, and at each step forward, the world moves with us.[22]

In the end it was his hopeful vision of the ascendancy of truth in history—itself rooted in his rarefied education—that secures Acton's place in the pantheon of high intellects.

---

[21] Acton, "The Study of History," in *SW* 2:552.

[22] Acton, "Notes on Archival Researches 1864–1868," ed. James C. Holland, in *Lord Acton. The Decisive Decade 1864–1874*, ed. Damian McElrath et al. (Louvain: Bibliothèque de l'Université & Publications Universitaires de Louvain, 1970), 139–40.

9

FREEDOM AND ORDER

Reflections from Lord Acton*

Samuel Gregg

INTRODUCTION

It would, of course, be an understatement to say that the primary motif of Lord Acton's life was a concern for human liberty. Throughout his years of scholarship, Acton wrote on an enormous variety of issues, including theology, philosophy, politics, church history, the state, nationalism, liberalism, conservatism, absolutism, democracy, reaction, and revolution. But the theme which links his hundreds of texts—letters, book reviews, journal articles, speeches, essays—is undoubtedly a concern for liberty. Acton even claimed that the history of liberty is "the only unity of the history of the world—and the one principle of a philosophy of history."[1]

Such a claim may seem strange to many of us today. But it reflects two things. One is what may be described as Acton's association with what some call "the Whig theory of history"—a theory which tends to view the past as reflecting an inevitable progression towards ever greater liberty and enlightenment.

---

*Address to Hanns-Seidel-Stiftung, Wildbad Kreuth, Germany, November 30, 2011.

[1] Add. Mss. 4991, p. 198, excerpted in *SW* 3:494.

153

The second is that Acton was very much a man of nineteenth-century Europe. This was a world in which liberalism, though hardly a monolithic movement, was perhaps one of the most influential forces shaping political and economic life. Nineteenth-century Western Europe, for example, witnessed a widening of political participation, relatively long periods of peace, an uneven but steady shift towards constitutionalism, and, perhaps above all, the spread of economic liberty and free trade across Europe and therefore the globe. All of these developments were associated with liberalism at this period of time.

But, we should note, nineteenth-century liberalism was not without its own complications. First, it was often associated with nationalism. As one of Acton's biographers writes, "Never was a liberal more isolated than Acton from the principles of his age, which applauded the victories that nationalism achieved all over Europe."[2] Second, liberalism increasingly encountered opposition in the form of the rise of socialist movements and Marxism. Third, liberalism was often associated with the violence and upheaval of the French Revolution. Fourth, at least in much of continental Europe, liberalism was often linked to deeply hostile attitudes towards Christianity in general, but Catholicism in particular.

Acton was one of the few self-identified European liberals who could address many of these complications. He was, after all, a cosmopolitan aristocrat and quite detached from many of his fellow liberals' nationalist opinions. As a devout Catholic, Acton did not share the implicit hostility of many European liberals to the church. Moreover, as an English Whig—and a very moderate one at that—Acton's liberalism was at least partially influenced by the thought of another Whig, Edmund Burke, widely regarded as one of the founders of modern conservatism.

Of course, Acton's thoughts on liberty are not without their own contradictions. Despite, for example, his insistence that Edmund Burke was "a teacher for Catholics"[3] and even "of mankind,"[4] Acton's

---

[2] Roland Hill, *Lord Acton* (New Haven: Yale University Press, 2000), 412.

[3] Acton to Richard Simpson, February 16, 1858, in *CLARS* 1:7.

[4] Acton, review of *History of the Life and Times of Edmund Burke*, by Thomas Macknight, *Rambler* n.s. (2nd ser.) 9 (April 1858): 268–73, here quoted from *SW* 1:140.

assessment of the French Revolution is far more positive than Burke's deeply negative view of the revolution. These apparent inconsistencies are also accompanied by, first, an unwillingness to give relatively clear answers to some important issues; second, the high degree of complexity that pervades some of Acton's interpretation of events; third, the fact that his thought was rarely presented in a detailed systematic form; and, fourth, an assumption that his readers are as familiar with the subjects he is addressing and their context as he is.

Such problems, of course, are hardly unique to Acton. It does mean, however, that Acton's answers to questions about freedom and order are never simple. But perhaps more significant is the way Acton's reflections on such subjects reflect his ability—which some have compared to that of Alexis de Tocqueville—to detect some of the deeper forces driving human history and how they either promoted freedom for individuals and society, or how they slowly diminished human liberty, without most people even realizing it.

Obviously I cannot do justice to the question of Acton's thinking about liberty and order here. That being the case, I would like to focus my attention upon two contributions from Acton that I regard as especially insightful for our thinking about freedom and order in twenty-first century Western societies. The first concerns the relationship between political liberty and democracy. The second is the relationship between political liberty and religion, or, more specifically, political liberty and Christianity.

POLITICAL LIBERTY AND DEMOCRACY

In identifying some of the characteristics of Acton's thinking about liberty and order, we need to be clear about what Acton understood by the expression *liberty*. Anyone who has read Acton's work soon realizes that, despite significant changes in his thinking over time, his attention remains very much upon the question of *political liberty*. Important questions such as the relationship between human reason, human will, and human emotions; the metaphysical dimension of freedom; or the philosophical anthropology of liberty receive relatively little attention in Acton's writings. In that sense, he does not engage with the same questions about human freedom that were central to the thought of figures such as Immanuel Kant and David

155

Hume, or, for that matter, Pope Leo XIII in his important but much neglected 1888 encyclical letter *Libertas*. But unlike these writers, we should remember, Acton was not a philosopher or theologian. He was first and foremost a historian.

By *political liberty*, Acton had in mind the freedom of individual human persons within a given political community. "By liberty," he wrote, "I mean the assurance that every man shall be protected in doing what he believes his duty against the influence of authority and majorities, custom and opinion."[5] It is through this lens that Acton approaches the issue of freedom and order as a historical and political question. Everything else—whether it is principles such as equality and national independence, or institutions such as property, rule of law, and democratic governance—is assessed from this standpoint in Acton's work.

Now, this does not mean that Acton was indifferent to the social, economic, and cultural problems that were beginning to impinge upon nineteenth-century political life. He was, for example, acutely aware of the rise of an urban industrial working class, something which prompted him to read several of Karl Marx's works. Nor, I should add, did Acton believe that normative issues such as the nature of human happiness or the moral culture of society were somehow beyond the scope of politics. Acton did, however, believe that we need to think about *how* these principles, institutions, and concerns can either contribute to—or impede—the development of political liberty.

When it came to the subject of the relationship between political liberty and democracy, Acton did believe that democracy can play a role in protecting political liberty insofar as he thought it generally unwise to entrust government to any one man or group. But Acton plainly had significant reservations about what the spread of democratic practices and emphases, such as universal suffrage and majority rule, might mean for the preservation and promotion of political liberty. He did not assume that the growth of democracy automatically expanded the scope of political liberty. He observed, for example, on several occasions that the test of political liberty in a given society could be assessed by considering how it treated minorities, especially

---

[5] Acton, "The History of Freedom in Antiquity," in *SW* 1:7.

unpopular minorities—and, as we know, democracies have not always treated such minorities especially well.

Political freedom, I suspect Acton would remind us today, is not the same thing as democracy. In this connection, Acton understood why Saint Thomas Aquinas occasionally used the Latin word *democratia* to describe unrestricted and above all arbitrary rule by ever-shifting majorities and why Aquinas used the expression *politica* to describe the notion of mixed government.

Many of these themes receive their fullest treatment in one of Acton's longer published papers: "The History of Freedom in Antiquity." In this lecture, Acton argues that Athenian democracy, under the inspiration of the philosopher Solon, represented a decisive break with what Acton calls the "universal degradation" of tyranny. For most of the ancient world's history, Acton argues, "rights secured by equal laws and by sharing power existed nowhere."[6] Solon, however, changed this by widening participation in government, and replacing the notion of government by compulsion with government by consent. To this extent, Acton believes that democracy—insofar as it diminishes the concentration of power—enhances political liberty. Solon, Acton also argues, regarded the essence of democracy as the principle that we have no master other than the law. From this standpoint, Acton sees a link between democracy and the growth of political liberty.

But as we read further into this same essay we realize that, while Acton sees positive aspects to democracy's emergence, he is not blind to democracy's potential threat to the idea of rule of law and its capacity to secure political liberty. Much turns, in Acton's view, on *how* democracies determine what constitutes just law and unjust law. In this regard, Acton believed that Athenian democracy was lacking inasmuch as there are other things besides majority consent that determine whether or not law is just or upholds political liberty. An essential characteristic of rule of law is non-arbitrary behavior on the part of the state, and there is no reason to assume that democracies will always act in a non-arbitrary manner.

The problem, Acton wrote, with fourth-century Athenian democracy was that the philosophy "in the ascendant taught them that there

---

[6] Acton, "The History of Freedom in Antiquity," in *SW* 1:9.

is no law superior to that of the State."[7] In this sense, Acton argues, democracies can indeed become tyrannical. "No authority in morals or in politics," Acton wrote, "remained unshaken by the motion that was in the air. No guide could be confidently trusted; there was no available criterion to appeal to, for the means of controlling or denying convictions that prevailed among the people. The popular sentiment as to what was right might be mistaken, but it was subject to no test. The people were, for practical purposes, the seat of the knowledge of good and evil."[8]

According to Acton, the only thing that held these arrangements together in fourth-century Athens was the influence of the statesman Pericles. Once Pericles died, Acton argues, Athenian democracy destroyed itself because it lacked authoritative reference points beyond the will of the majority. "It is bad," Acton suggests, "to be oppressed by a minority, but it is worse to be oppressed by a majority. For there is a reserve of latent power in the masses which, if it is called into play, the minority can seldom resist."[9] Alexis de Tocqueville develops a very similar argument in the second volume of his *Democracy in America*.

Today, most of us in the West live in constitutional democracies in which there exist considerable checks upon democratic majoritarianism. Acton himself points out that the intellectual and institutional roots of many of these limitations, such as the idea of a separation of powers, are to be found in the medieval period. That said, it is hard to dispute that tendencies to view majority opinion as the ultimate justification for any number of positions are very widespread in our societies. This is perhaps especially true in societies where utilitarian and positivist conceptions of law, morality, and the nature of the state are especially influential.

The question for modern democracies, from Acton's standpoint, thus becomes one of how we can preserve political liberty from being crushed by majorities. Do we have to simply hope that we will always be able to find figures such as Pericles? Or do we eventually find ourselves having to restrict the power of democratic norms and institutions so much that their legitimacy becomes extremely ques-

---

[7] Acton, "The History of Freedom in Antiquity," in *SW* 1:13.

[8] Acton, "The History of Freedom in Antiquity," in *SW* 1:12.

[9] Acton, "The History of Freedom in Antiquity," in *SW* 1:13.

tionable? To Acton's mind, this issue of how we maintain a social and political order of freedom eventually leads us to consider the relationship between political liberty and religion.

POLITICAL LIBERTY AND CHRISTIANITY

The role played by religion in Acton's own life is perhaps best described as complicated. What, however, is not in doubt is Acton's conviction that religion—by which he meant, first, Judaism but then above all Christianity—had played an indispensible role in both promoting and ordering human freedom and political liberty.

Though Acton did not hesitate to underline the failings of Christians throughout the centuries, this theme of Christianity's direct and indirect contributions to the cause of ordered liberty pervades the corpus of Acton's writings. No doubt, it owes something to his effort to reconcile the forces of liberalism—perhaps moderate Whiggery is a better word for what Acton has in mind—with the other great love of his life: his Catholic faith. Yet Acton is also very clear that his attention to Christianity's contribution to political liberty owes much to his conviction that freedom is bound to play a major role in human history because of its direct relationship to the workings of Providence.

This point is underscored by Acton's paper on the "History of Freedom in Antiquity," but perhaps even more in his other famous paper, "The History of Freedom in Christianity." In his paper on freedom and antiquity, Acton claims that the preservation of freedom was the concern of some, especially among some figures associated with ancient Israel as well as various Stoic thinkers of ancient Greece. Acton insists, however, that political liberty was never quite able to make the type of intellectual and cultural breakthrough in the pre-Christian ancient world that was needed if freedom was to become a primary reference point for political life. Acton observes that we do find the notion that there is a higher law that the state cannot transgress in the thought of pre-Christian ancient philosophers such as Socrates, Plato, and Aristotle. By this, Acton presumably means the natural law. Acton's point, however, is that this vital constraint on the power of the state—be it the polis of ancient Greece or the vast empires that dominated the Middle East—was, in a sense, "stuck" beneath the pre-Christian world's expectations, institutions, and, perhaps above all, pagan religious cultures. "If I may employ an expressive anachronism," Acton adds, "the vice of the classic State was that it was both Church and State in one."[10] The idea of a higher law to which all of us—including the state—are answerable was therefore unable to permeate the wider cultures of the ancient world.

That the advent of Christianity fundamentally changed this situation is one of the major themes pervading Acton's "History of Freedom in Christianity." Christianity is, to Acton's mind, what permitted the idea of human freedom to escape from previously insurmountable obstacles. Jesus Christ's famous words recorded in the Gospel of Saint Luke, "render to Caesar the things that are Caesar's, and to God the things that are God's" (Luke 20:25), were literally revolutionary in their implications for how most people (including non-Christians) subsequently understood the nature of the state and its relationship with political liberty. With good reason, Luke's Gospel records that "they [his questioners] marvel[ed] at his answer" (Luke 20:26). For, as Acton observes "in religion, morality, and politics there was only one legislator and one authority" in the pre-Christian ancient world: the *pólis* (πόλις) and later the Roman state.[11] Separation of the temporal and spiritual was incomprehensible to pagan minds because a distinction between the "temporal" and "spiritual" did not exist in the pre-Christian world. Christ's words effectively asserted the liberty of the spiritual authority from the political in all matters of faith, worship, and morals.

This was a new departure in the world's experience of religion. As Acton well knew, the state had controlled religion in all its aspects in the pagan world. The kingdom of God that Christ had announced was spiritual, but it required independence as a social organization so that the things of God could be given at least equal seriousness to those of Caesar. When events led to conflict with the state on this issue, and the Christians faced martyrdom, the political effects in theory and in practice did much to determine the shape of European political culture and through it that of the modern world.

By universalizing the Jewish belief that those exercising legal authority were as subject to Yahweh's law as everyone else, Christianity

---

[10] Acton, "The History of Freedom in Antiquity," in *SW* 1:17.

[11] Acton, "The History of Freedom in Antiquity," in *SW* 1:17–18.

achieved the hitherto unthinkable: the state's de-sacralization, but without destroying social order. Certainly, Christianity was respectful of the Roman state's authority. The writings of Saint Paul and Saint Peter, for instance, underlined the divine origin of the state's legal authority. Nevertheless, Judaism and Christianity also quietly insisted that Caesar was not a god and may not behave as if he was god. Though Jews and Christians would pray *for* earthly rulers, it was anathema for Jews and Christians to pray *to* such rulers. While Jews and Christians regarded the state as the custodian of social order, they did not consider the state itself to be the ultimate source of truth and law. When Constantine gave religious liberty to the Christian church in his Edict of Milan (AD 313), he did not subject Christianity to himself. Instead Constantine effectively declared that Caesar was no longer god. As Acton writes, "nobody warned [Constantine] that by promoting the Christian religion he was tying one of his hands, and surrendering the prerogative of the Caesars."[12]

Acton's point, however, is not simply one of the church's existence and its particular claims placing a radical limit upon the state's ability to coerce its citizens and subjects. As I mentioned, Acton regarded liberty as a *providential* idea. Freedom is, to his mind, willed and protected by God himself. It therefore plays the same role in human history that Tocqueville attributed to equality. According to Acton, however, freedom precedes equality in the divine order of values, and is therefore superior to it. From Acton's standpoint, this means that we have reason to believe that political freedom is something that *cannot*—no matter how hard humans might try—ever be utterly suppressed to the point of permanent extinction.

This does not mean, of course, that the spread and growth of political liberty does not encounter difficulties. But in Acton's view, periods of struggle, servitude, and bondage serve their own role in helping us to better understand the importance of political liberty as well as the conditions and institutions that promote and order it. The primary example that Acton provides of this in his "History of Freedom in Christianity" is the constant struggle between the church and the ambitions of secular feudal lords throughout the Middle Ages. This historical period witnessed constant attempts by feudal

---

[12] Acton, "The History of Freedom in Christianity," in *SW* 1:30.

lords to subordinate the independence of the church. If, Acton wrote, the church's liberty in the West had been "terminated" by a victory of temporal powers, he believed that "all Europe would have sunk down under a Byzantine or Muscovite despotism."[13]

It was not, Acton states, that the church consciously chose to align itself with the cause of political liberty. Acton is clear that general political liberty is not the end for which the church strived during this period. Instead, Acton's point is that once the church's liberty (*libertas ecclesiae*) from the control of secular rulers had been formally accepted, the application of the principle to other spheres of life could not be stopped. If the church was free, many asked, then why should not other groups and individuals enjoy similar freedom under the law as well as liberty from excessive state or lordly control?

It is, Acton claims, at least partially because of the church's cease-less struggle for freedom from state control that "the towns of Italy and Germany won their franchises, France got her States-General, and England her Parliament out of the alternate phases of the con-test." And, Acton adds, "as long as it lasted it prevented the rise of divine right." Indeed, Acton suggests that the church's struggle helped solidify the idea "of the divine right of the people to raise up and pull down their princes." *Vox populi Vox Dei.*[14]

As a consequence, Acton generally has high praise for the politi-cal arrangements that gradually prevailed during the Middle Ages. "Representative government," he claims, "was almost universal. The methods of election were crude; but the principle that no tax was lawful that was not granted by the class that paid it—that is, that taxa-tion was inseparable from representation—was recognized, not as the privilege of certain countries, but as the right of all.... Slavery was almost everywhere extinct; and absolute power was deemed more intolerable and more criminal than slavery. The right of insurrection was not only admitted but defined, as a duty sanctioned by religion. Even the principles of the Habeas Corpus Act, and the method of the Income Tax, were already known.... The political produce of the Middle Ages was a system of states in which authority was restricted by the representation of powerful classes, by privileged associations,

---

[13] Acton, "The History of Freedom in Christianity," in *SW* 1:33.

[14] Acton, "The History of Freedom in Christianity," in *SW* 1:33.

and by the acknowledgment of duties superior to those which are imposed by man."[15]

No doubt, there are many who would dispute aspects of Acton's analysis of this period. Then there are those who persist in caricaturing the Middle Ages as a time of darkness and despotism. But whatever one thinks of these critiques and mythologies, Acton does provide a useful corrective to popular misconceptions of the role of medieval Christianity in promoting political liberty, albeit usually in indirect ways. Here it is also worth mentioning that Acton was also one of the first nineteenth-century thinkers to draw attention to how Saint Thomas Aquinas' articulation of the natural-law tradition played a critical role in promoting human liberty. Oddly enough, however, Acton neglected to point out that it was Aquinas' conception of human flourishing and how it occurs that underscored Aquinas' insistence upon the need to limit state power, rather than any *a priori* concern for political liberty.

Acton's view of the post-Reformation contribution of Christianity to political liberty is much more mixed. He suggests, for example, that the sixteenth-century religious schisms contributed in particular ways to the growth of state absolutism and the gradual breakdown of many of the institutions and constitutional principles that had hitherto protected political liberty. In Acton's words, "religion, instead of emancipating the nations, had become an excuse for the criminal acts of despots. Calvin preached and Bellarmine lectured, but Machiavelli reigned."[16] In other words, the collapse in religious unity, the growing emphasis upon nationality, and the emergence of doctrines such as the divine right of kings led to the growth of state power and the use of state power against Catholic and Protestant Christian alike, but also anyone inclined to resist the march of absolutism.

From Acton's standpoint, the modern sovereign nation-states which began emerging in the late Middle Ages went much further than medieval lords in their efforts to subordinate the autonomy of religious organizations. In a number of Protestant nation-states such as England and the Scandinavian nations, the monarch claimed to be the unrivaled and uncontested head of the church, answerable to

---

[15] Acton, "The History of Freedom in Christianity," in *SW* 1:36–37.

[16] Acton, "The History of Freedom in Christianity," in *SW* 1:40.

God alone within the boundaries of their state. To varying degrees, national identity in such nations became partly associated with membership in the national church. In Catholic nation-states, the spiritual allegiance of the Catholic Church to the pope in his capacity as bishop of Rome and successor of Saint Peter made this goal of subordination much harder for monarchs to achieve. Nonetheless, temporal Catholic rulers such as Louis XIV and the Spanish Habsburg and Bourbon monarchs did not hesitate to claim a certain, albeit limited authority over the church within their realms.

In keeping, however, with his insistence that liberty is a providential idea, Acton argues that one result of the persecution and growth in state power associated with the Reformation was a gradual realization that religious liberty is "the generating principle of civil [liberty], and that civil liberty is the necessary condition of religious [liberty]." Only by limiting the authority of the state, it was realized, can "the liberty of Churches ... be assured."[17] In other words, Acton argues, it was "divisions in religion" which "forced toleration," and religious toleration implied a tremendous limitation of state power and therefore a renewed boost to political freedom.[18]

By religious liberty and religious toleration, it is clear that Acton does not have in mind religious indifferentism, either on the part of individuals or the state. Nor does he have in mind the idea of religious liberty associated with the French Revolution which, we should note, was promoted by many nineteenth-century continental liberals: that is, the severe limitation of religious activity. Instead, Acton appears, albeit rather vaguely, to anticipate the understanding of religious liberty as articulated at the Second Vatican Council: immunity from coercion in matters of religious belief and action, consistent with the legitimate demands of public order, in order that people might be free to pursue and know religious truth. For if religion is conceptualized in this manner, then religious liberty is not protecting or promoting religious indifferentism or relativism. Instead religious liberty is primarily about seeking to guarantee that all are *free to consider* whether or not there is an ultimate transcendent being whose existence provides a compelling explanation of life, and then to assent to the conclusions

---

[17] Acton, "The History of Freedom in Christianity," in *SW* 1:47.

[18] Acton, "The History of Freedom in Christianity," in *SW* 1:53.

of their reason. This is crucial for the *integrity* of one's religious belief or non-belief. As Saint Augustine wrote: "If there is no assent, there is no faith, for without assent one does not really believe."[19]

CONCLUSION

And so, to conclude: Acton's reflections upon political liberty and its relationship to democracy as well as to religion are obviously conditioned by some particularly nineteenth-century European concerns. That means, of course, that we should be careful about asking ourselves what their significance for political liberty might be in our own time.

When it comes to restraining the capacity of democracy to undermine political liberty, Acton was inclined to believe, especially towards the end of his life, that the system of federalism offered "the true natural check on absolute democracy." In this regard, he described America's federalism as "the one immortal tribute of America to political science."[20] Acton was, we should note, writing at a time when federalism had become very unfashionable in Europe and perceived as an obstacle to centrally-driven economic, political, and military development. It is my suspicion that, in light of all the damage to political liberty caused by political and economic centralization throughout the twentieth century, Acton would be disappointed by how little attention federalism receives today as a way of ensuring democracy does not dissolve into majoritarian rule.

Concerning the issue of political liberty and religion, and specifically Christianity, I suspect Acton would be surprised by the contemporary tendency to treat religion and its relationship to freedom primarily in sociological terms. To a certain extent, Acton's work as a historian inclined him in that direction. But, as we have seen, Acton's approach as a historian was also influenced by his willingness to take the impact of religious, theological, and moral *ideas* and *values* seriously.

Because for all his efforts to turn the study of history into a type of science, Acton was no positivist. Nor was he a moral or religious

---

[19] Augustine, *Enchiridion*, ch. 20.
[20] Acton, *LFR*, 37; *SW* 1:211.

relativist. Freedom was no mere subjective value for Acton, precisely because it was, in his view, willed by God for humanity. For the same reason, Acton was also convinced that freedom was nothing else but the right to do what one ought, and that part of the purpose of the study of history is to teach us how to distinguish between the oughts and the ought-nots—or between the order and disorder—knowable through revelation and reason. In that regard, Acton maintained that there exists a universal moral code—based on the Decalogue and natural law—which Christianity had played a major role in transmitting to humanity. How else could we understand Acton's statement in his inaugural address at Cambridge that "opinions alter, manners change, creeds rise and fall, but the moral law is written on the tablets of eternity."[21] In a twenty-first century world in which the prevailing tendency is to limit affirmation of the truth to that which is scientifically verifiable, such statements seem almost anachronistic. To Acton's mind, however, they reflect his conviction that the fact of human liberty points to something greater that itself, without which freedom itself, he believed, would have no order and make no sense.

---

[21] Acton, *LMH*, 27; *SW* 1:551.

About the Contributors

Josef L. Altholz (1933–2003) taught history at the University of Minnesota for over forty years. During his distinguished academic career he was a founding member and the second president of the Research Society for Victorian Periodicals, served as president of the American Catholic Historical Society (1986–1987), and was coeditor of *The Correspondence of Lord Acton and Richard Simpson* (1971–1975).

Christoph Böhr is Professor of Contemporary Philosophy and a fellow at the Institute for Philosophy at the Phil.-Theol. Hochschule Benedikt XVI. Heiligenkreuz in Vienna. He is also a permanent fellow of the Collegium Artes Liberales / Institute for Advanced Studies in the Humanities and the Social Sciences at Vytautas Magnus Universität. He is the editor of the series Das Bild vom Menschen und die Ordnung der Gesellschaft (Springer, 2011–) and the author of many books, including *Der Maßstab der Menschenwürde. Christlicher Glaube, ethischer Anspruch und politisches Handeln* (2003), *Gesellschaft neu denken* (2004), and *Gewissen und Politik* (2006).

Owen Chadwick (1916–2015) was one of the twentieth century's most respected church historians. He was named Dixie Professor of Ecclesiastical History at Cambridge University in 1958, and in 1968 he was elected Regius Professor of Modern History, the same chair that Lord Acton once held. Chadwick wrote many significant studies of the church and individuals in the modern era, including *The Secularization of the European Mind in the Nineteenth Century* (1975), *The Spirit of the Oxford Movement* (1990), *Acton and History* (1998), and *A History of the Popes, 1830–1914* (1998).

Samuel Gregg is Director of Research at the Acton Institute. He has written and spoken extensively on political economy, economic history, ethics in finance, and natural-law theory. Among his many books are *On Ordered Liberty* (2003), *The Modern Papacy* (2009), and *For God and Profit: How Banking and Finance Can Serve the Common Good* (2016). He is a member of the Royal Historical Society, the Mont Pelerin Society, the Philadelphia Society, and the Royal Economic Society.

James C. Holland is Professor Emeritus of History at Shepherd University, where he has taught since 1971. He is coeditor of *The Correspondence of Lord Acton and Richard Simpson* (1971–1975) and the author of *A Capital in Search of a Nation* (1986) and *Shenandoah Valley Memories of the War Between the States* (1992).

Russell Kirk (1918–1994), historian, social philosopher, and critic, wrote on subjects ranging from literature and the history of ideas to problems of education and culture, producing during his long career thirty-two books, hundreds of essays, a syndicated newspaper column, and several works of fiction. Kirk was awarded the Presidential Citizens Medal in 1989, and was a Constitutional Fellow of the National Endowment for the Humanities, a Senior Fellow of the American Council of Learned Societies, and a Fulbright lecturer in Scotland. Among his many books are *The Conservative Mind* (1953), *Edmund Burke: A Genius Reconsidered* (1967), and *Enemies of the Permanent Things* (1969).

Johann Christian Koecke is Educational Coordinator in the Political Education Forum at the Konrad-Adenauer-Stiftung in Sankt Augustin, Germany. In addition to various essays—including others on Lord Acton—he is the author of *Zeit des Ressentiments, Zeit der Erlösung. Nietzsches Typologie temporaler Interpretation und ihre Aufhebung in der Zeit* (1994).

Made in the USA
Lexington, KY
27 May 2017

Stephen J. Tonsor (1923–2014) taught history for forty years at the University of Michigan, where he received the Distinguished Teacher Award in 1962. His doctoral research focused on Ignaz von Döllinger and modern European history, but during his academic career he wrote on a wide variety of topics including education, equality, politics, and American culture. His writings include many articles and reviews, *Tradition and Reform in Education* (1974), and *Equality, Decadence, and Modernity* (2005).

Rudolf Uertz is Professor Extraordinarius of Political Science at the Katholischen Universität Eichstätt-Ingolstadt. From 1985 to 1991 he was Lecturer in Social Ethics at the Universität Siegen. He has written extensively on the history and relationship between Christianity and democracy. His books include *Christentum und Sozialismus in der frühen CDU* (1981), *Christliche Demokratie im zusammenwachsenden Europa* (coedited with Günter Buchstab, 2004), and *Vom Gottesrecht zum Menschenrecht. Das katholische Staatsdenken in Deutschland von der Französischen Revolution bis zum II. Vatikanischen Konzil (1789–1965)* (2005).

64072294R00106

Made in the USA
Lexington, KY
27 May 2017